SEEING THE HAND OF GOD

Judith A. Kohlasch

TRILOGY

Trilogy Christian Publishers

A Wholly Owned Subsidiary of Trinity Broadcasting Network

2442 Michelle Drive

Tustin, CA 92780

For information, address Trilogy Christian Publishing Rights
Department, 2442 Michelle Drive, Tustin, CA 92780.

Trilogy Christian Publishing/ TBN and colophon are trademarks of
Trinity Broadcasting Network.

For information about special discounts for bulk purchases, please contact Trilogy Christian Publishing.

Trilogy Disclaimer: The views and content expressed in this book are those of the author and may not necessarily reflect the views and doctrine of Trilogy Christian Publishing or the Trinity Broadcasting Network.

10 9 8 7 6 5 4 3 2 1

Library of Congress Cataloging-in-Publication Data is available.

ISBN 979-8-89333-079-3

ISBN 979-8-89333-080-9 (ebook)

SEEING THE HAND OF GOD
By Judith A. Kohlasch

INTRODUCTION

Growing up in an abusive, dysfunctional home caused serious psychological issues in my life that manifested physically, emotionally, and socially. From an early age, I knew about God and continually wondered where He was and why He wasn't fixing anything or stopping the abuse. I prayed and prayed, and my prayers were never answered in the way I wanted them answered. Then God was banned in the home, I fell away and took the path I thought was best for me, only to realize how wrong I was.

I got tossed, like the waves and the wind, in every direction people directed me. I finally searched for the one and only true God, not the gods most people tell you about. I found Him at thirty years old, or should I say, He found me, and He has truly transformed me.

Once my eyes were opened, I was able to see where God intervened in my life and where God was using past hurts and wrongs for His glory and blessing me at the same time. This book is only an inkling of what I have seen and been blessed with.

None of my family members or individuals mentioned or discussed were consulted about this book's content other than Annette Sarah Kohlasch, my daughter, as this book is about my feelings, my emotions, my perceptions, and my life. The names of everyone other than Annette and Theo Warren Kohlasch, my deceased husband, have been changed to protect their privacy and confidentiality. Theo was a part of my life for over thirty-seven years, and I'm sorry he's not here to see God's purpose fulfilled in my life, even though he never stopped pushing me to get this book written.

This book is dedicated to Annette Sarah Kohlasch, my loving daughter, who is my miracle child and one of the greatest blessings in my life. With God's love and direction, I have been blessed to watch Annette grow into a fierce, strong, stable, dedicated, focused, and professional young woman. I cannot wait to see God's purpose being fulfilled in her life, as she has been a part of God's purpose for my life. God loves you, Annette Sarah Kohlasch, and I love you too! Never stop looking to God for all the answers and blessings you need in your life. God will always be with you and for you, no matter what happens in life.

CHAPTER ONE–
THE TENDER YEARS

PURE WHITE LILIES

At an early age, Mom would tell me she never wanted me because I was the product of rape by my father. I was too young to know what that meant. I only knew I needed to find a way to get Mom to love me. If not Mom, then I needed to find another loving mother, loving father, or other people who would love me. I believed the sentiment and the song saying, "All you need is love!"

Searching for people to love me began first in my neighborhood. There were lots of children my age, especially young girls. I remember telling myself I could have lots of friends who would love me.

The "mean" neighbor across the street did not like children. He screamed and yelled at us, and I didn't understand why. I only learned to avoid him.

Next, there was this "nice" older gentleman. I thought he looked like what a father or grandfather figure would look like. Since my father died of lung cancer when I was one year old, I did not know what a father should look like other than seeing some of the neighborhood fathers. I remember whenever I went outside to play, I ran over to this man's house to see if he was in the yard tending his beautiful garden. He had the most wonderful flowers in that garden, including roses and lilies.

Then, one Easter morning before church, I wanted to go outside.

"Mom, may we go out front before we head to church?"

"Yes, but do not get your clothes dirty."

"Okay."

I saw Mr. Edward outside his house. He was doing his daily check on his flowers and plants, and I immediately ran over.

"Hi, Mr. Edward, what ya doing?"

"Pruning my lilies and picking some for Easter," said Mr. Edward without looking up from his plants.

"Look at me," twisting from side to side in my snow-white, flowery Easter dress, barely visible over the tops of his blossoming lilies. I felt beautiful.

"Take my picture, Mr. Edward. Can I pull weeds after church?" I asked as I jumped out from the lily plants. Mr. Edward would give me $.50 for a box of weeds.

Mom would constantly say, "Everyone will work to help pay the bills. I cannot do this on my own." Money, or the lack thereof, always stoked fights in the house. So my thinking was, if I could pull weeds and get money from Mr. Edward, I could help pay the bills.

"Maybe later when you are in shorts and a shirt," replied Mr. Edward.

"Okay, see you later." I headed home to join my family for Easter Mass.

At that age, I did not know the things that Mr. Edward would eventually do to me in his shed were considered inappropriate touches. These same kinds of things were happening at home when the next-door neighbor's teenage boys would come over to spend time with my two older brothers. Things that went on in my house were not okay.

After Easter Mass, I changed my clothes.

"Mom, can we go outside and play?"

"Yes, get out of the house. I need some time to myself." Mom did not seem to like all of us children around.

Off we went outside to play. We spent a great deal of time outside playing with neighbor children.

In those years, video games did not exist, and cell phones didn't exist. We had a landline telephone attached to the wall with a cord. Our black-and-white television played only five or six broadcast local channels, and we were only allowed to watch TV on Saturdays when all our chores were done or when Mom wanted us to see something special during the week.

I remembered Mr. Edward said I could pull weeds after church and make money, so I immediately headed to his house to find him. I did not see him outside of his house, so I walked up his driveway to the back of his house to see if I could find him.

I found Mr. Edward working in his shed at the back of his house. I went in.

"Hello," he said, "I was wondering if you were coming over after church. Come here and let me hug you. Sit on my lap." I did not know any better, so I did.

"You know I love you."

This was all I wanted to hear.

He continued, "When people love you, they make you feel good. Does this feel good to you?" Mr. Edward would ask as he was doing inappropriate touching.

I did not know if he ever did these things with my siblings or other children in my neighborhood. No one ever talked about these things, and I sure did not because he said it was "our secret."

Little did I, as a five-year-old innocent child, know that the man who grew those beautiful pure white lilies and lovely roses had allowed the worst kind of spiritual wickedness to take over his life. I thought it was "love" because that is what he called it. I ignored everything that went on with Mr. Edward, except knowing I could make $.50 a box if I pulled weeds for him. I could help pay the bills, and Mom would be happy. The other stuff did not matter until I was old enough to understand it *did* matter when I began experiencing the negative consequences in my life.

As 1 John 2:16 (NLT) says, "For everything in the world—the lust of the flesh, the lust of the eyes, and the pride of life—comes not from the Father but from the world." Looking back, it was clear that Mr. Edward did not know he was following

Satan or did not care. First Peter 5:8 (NLT) says, "Stay alert! Watch out for your great enemy, the devil. He prowls around like a roaring lion, looking for someone to devour." I had been consumed by a man who allowed Satan to use him to commit evil acts on children.

In Psalm 37:10 (TLV), it says, "Yet a little while, and the wicked will be no more. Yes, you will look at his place, but he will not be there." I am not sure how long this went on, but eventually, Mr. Edward died as he was quite elderly when I first met him. I was sad that I had lost someone who said he loved me, but glad that those uncomfortable things he did were no longer happening. I'm not sure if Mom ever knew what was going on there.

ABUSIVE MOTHER VS. ADULTEROUS WOMAN

"Okay, where did you get the money to buy all that candy?" Mom yelled angrily, glaring at each of us six children. "You will tell me, or no one is moving from here."

I'm not sure how old I was.

But I do remember this being one of the earliest memories of my not-so-great childhood.

I knew I truly did not know where the money had come from. I was getting dressed for the day, and there it was, in my bottom dresser drawer. In my youthful mindset, I had wanted to make my siblings happy, so I took the money and showed it to them.

"Let's go to the country club and buy some candy," said one of my siblings.

So off we went to the country club near the house. We proudly walked up to the counter, placed the $20.00 bill on the counter, and said:

"I want Blow Pops."

"I want Necco wafers."

"I want Bazooka bubble gum."

"I want Sweeties."

"I want Pixie Straws."

Down the line, we each voiced our wants. We haggled with the clerk until we all got something we wanted, and there was even some spare change to bring home. The clerk placed the candy in a brown bag, and we went home.

Upon arriving home, we went straight into the girls' bedroom while ripping open candy wrappers as fast as we could.

I could not understand why we were told to hide our treasures from Mom. But not knowing anything to the contrary, into the room we went. We were devouring all the different candies we had bought when Mom walked in.

Busted!

"Where did the money for this candy come from? Who took the money from my purse? I am missing money from my purse."

At that moment, it was every child for themselves, and because I had found the money and presented it to my siblings, it was all my fault. This, however, did not satisfy Mom. Mom wanted the full truth and how it had come to happen.

We were all lined up in a row. And down the row, she went aggressively spanking us, one by one, until someone confessed to stealing the money. Finally, after what felt like days but realistically was only a couple of hours, one of my siblings confessed to the truth. This sibling believed that because I was the "favorite child," if the transgression were ever discovered, Mom would not do anything much about it. However, my sibling was wrong, very wrong, and although I have forgiven them for this, it is not something that can be forgotten.

One of Mom's favorite punishments was to tell us to kneel on the hard floor near the end of her bed and ask God for forgiveness for what we had done wrong. Some of these kneeling punishments would last for an hour to two, depending on Mom's mood. We were not allowed to rest on our heels or stretch out our legs. To this day, I cannot kneel without excruciating pain and great difficulty getting up. Kneeling became synonymous with punishment and not worship for God even though Mom would have us recite The Lord's Prayer found in Matthew 6:9–13 (KJV): "...Our Father which art in heaven, Hallowed be thy name. Thy kingdom come. Thy will be done in earth, as it is in heaven. Give us this day our daily bread. And forgive us our debts, as we forgive our debtors. And lead us not into temptation, but deliver us from evil: For thine is the kingdom, and the power, and the glory, for ever. Amen." She wanted us to ask God for provisions and, more importantly, for forgiveness for the "evil" we had done.

. . .

As the years passed, the physical, emotional, and verbal abuse continued well into my college years and during my marriage. The accompanying thoughts and feelings became so ingrained into me that I thought I deserved it, thereby spending years of my life wrongfully enabling this kind of behavior and attitude.

Regretfully, my mother had not learned the importance of Ephesians 6:4 (NLT): "Fathers, do not provoke your children to anger by the way you treat them. Rather, bring them up with the discipline and instruction that comes from the Lord." I read that in the Bible numerous times and used it to justify my unrighteous anger and fits of uncontrollable rage in my life, blaming my mother.

There was a point late in Mom's life when I questioned her about why she did the things she did to us. This was when the truth was finally revealed. Mom had been abandoned by her mother and an older sister who was nine years older than her. When her mother died, Mom's older sister did not want to be the "woman-servant" of the house, so she left. Mom was left to grow up on the farm with her father. She endured physical abuse from her father, as she was the only "woman-servant" in the house, and her father wanted her to clean the house and take care of him. There was one problem. Mom was five years old at the time.

During this time, my grandfather had a moonshine still on the farm which he was no longer using. It was the era of prohibition. His next-door neighbor asked him to use the still to make moonshine since he wasn't using it, and my grandfather said okay. Due to the usage of the still and the placement of it on my grandfather's property, he was the one who suffered the blame and was subsequently arrested for making moonshine and put in jail, and Mom, who was still a minor, was placed in foster care. Between my grandfather's home and her new foster home, Mom became and remained the family servant. Abuse was the only thing Mom knew. She never experienced unconditional love from her parents. She never learned any differently, so she raised us the only way she knew how.

Before learning about Mom's childhood, I wanted to let everyone know what she was doing to us. I wanted to have her arrested for the abuse she put us through, but I loved Mom in the only way I knew how. I believed Mark 7:10 (NIV), which said, "For Moses said, 'Honor your father and mother,' and, 'Anyone who curses their father or mother is to be put to death.'" I did not want to be put to death, but I did not understand why Mom was so mean. I thought it was my fault because I was not good enough or did not do enough good things for Mom and that's why she didn't love me. Romans 3:10–12 (NLT) says, "No one is righteous—not even one. No one is truly wise; no one is seeking God. All have turned away; all have become useless. No one does good, not a single one." Not knowing or understanding the Word of God or the Good News, I believed I deserved everything I got.

Since then, many years later, my walk with Christ has shown me that my prideful, righteous self was no different than the Pharisees who caught the woman committing adultery and brought her to the public square where Jesus was. They demanded that she be stoned to death, the penalty for committing adultery, according to the law.

When Jesus said, "he who has no sin should cast the first stone," they all walked away. I could not cast the first stone at Mom because I was in no position to judge her for her sinful actions because I myself had my own sinful actions. John 8:7–11 (NIV) says, "Let any one of you who is without sin be the first to throw a stone at her. Again he stooped down and wrote on the ground." At this, those who heard began to go away one at a time, the older ones first, until only Jesus was left, with the woman still standing there. Jesus straightened up and asked her, 'Woman, where are they? Has no one condemned you?' 'No one, sir,' she said. 'Then neither do I condemn you,' Jesus declared. 'Go now and leave your life of sin.'"

Looking back to that childhood memory and the subsequent conversation with Mom, I now know that through the salvation of Jesus Christ, I can live a life believing Romans 8:1 (NLT), "So now there is no condemnation for those who belong to Christ Jesus."

I also learned that God was there for both my mother and me. As stated in Psalm 68:5 (NIV), God was "A father to the fatherless [me] and a defender of widows [Mom] is God in his holy dwelling." The problem was Mom and I didn't know how to reach Him at the time.

CATHOLIC SCHOOL

I was born into a family of nine siblings. There were two half-sisters and one half-brother from my father's first marriage.

Mom had her first marriage to an army soldier during World War II, which only lasted for nine months. I do not know if it was annulled or if it ended in divorce. However, Mom never talked about it with any of the other siblings except me. The other siblings found out about him when she was in hospice care, right before she passed away.

After the end of Mom's first marriage, she met my father, got married, and had six children: three boys and three girls. My father died when I was one year old, which left her alone with six children under the age of eight.

I attended a Catholic school from kindergarten to fourth grade. I only have a few memories other than uniforms, nuns with dangerous rulers used daily on students, and lots of expensive schoolbooks. Luckily, with all my siblings, I was able to use some of their recycled schoolbooks, and Mom saved some money there.

The Catholic school taught me there was a long list of rules to follow in order to be accepted and loved by God and others. I later learned this paralleled the "Mosaic Law."

One day, when I was in kindergarten, Mom picked us up from school. When we got home, she told us something horrible happened to the country.

"President John F. Kennedy was killed today. He was assassinated."

I could not quite understand what "assassinated" or "killed" meant because I had never experienced anyone who was assassinated or killed. I knew my father was dead, and he wasn't around anymore, but he wasn't "assassinated" or "killed." He just got sick and died.

That night after dinner, Mom sat us all down in the living room in front of our black-and-white TV. We watched the evening news reports and tried to understand what had happened to our great country. The reports went on for days leading up to and including the President's funeral. We watched some of them after we finished our homework. This was my first encounter with someone being killed. However, it wasn't anybody I knew.

At school, I remember wearing blue-striped uniforms that went down to my knee, which was good because they covered welts and/or bruises on my body received during punishment at home. I remember one day, I bent over to pick up something that dropped, and the nun said in a disturbing voice,

"Judy, come here, please."

I had no idea what I had done wrong. I was scared. Was I going to get into trouble and have to explain it to Mom?

I slowly slinked to the nun's desk. With me facing the classroom, she discreetly hiked up my skirt in the back so no one would see anything.

The nun, speaking softly into my ear, asked me, "What are those welts and bruises on the back of your thighs? Where did they come from?"

"What welts and bruises? I do not know what you are talking about?"

The nun sent me to the head office with a note. When I got there, I was asked again:

"What are these bruises and welts on your thighs? Where did they come from?"

I had to think up a good excuse because I knew if the truth ever came out, Mom would be fired from her job working in the school cafeteria where we received reduced meals. Or, even worse, Mom would be taken away from us, and all of us could be placed in foster care. Mom wasn't the best mom, but she was the only parent we had.

"Oh, those. I was playing outside with my siblings, and I fell on a stack of metal pipes at the golf course and hurt my backside and thighs."

It appeared to work because I was sent back to my classroom.

When I was six years old, I remember worrying constantly about Mom dying. I was afraid my siblings and I would become orphans. I remember when Mom's sister visited, she told us no one would want us if anything happened to Mom. She also told us that few, if any, people in the world would take six children together. Therefore, all of us would be split up because she would not take us in, no matter what. She did not think highly of her nieces and nephews and always put down her sister.

Mom was incredibly angry with God because God let her husband die, and she didn't want to raise all these children alone. Mom was scared and lonely.

Mom tried to kill herself twice with an overdose. Both times, someone in the family contacted the Catholic church. They sent over priests to speak with Mom. I did not know the full extent of what happened, but I do remember the priests going into Mom's room and spending several hours with her because she was sick. I remember crying and praying Mom would get well and the priests would heal her or, if they could not, ask God to heal her. I assume the priests kept Mom's suicide attempts secret from law enforcement and child services because we were never removed from the home. I think they understood that there were too many children, and Mom promised to take care of us.

Psalm 68:6 (TLV) says, "A father of orphans, defender of widows, is God in His holy dwelling." I'm not sure if Mom knew or believed that God was there all those years for her as a widow, nor if we knew or believed that God was there for all of us siblings who were fatherless. Whether we knew it or not, God was there. Our foundation may have been rocky, but he held us together and guided us. Psalm 40:1–2 (NLT) confirms this. "I waited patiently for the Lord to help me, and he turned to me and heard my cry. He lifted me out of the pit of despair, out of the mud and the mire. He set my feet on solid ground and steadied me as I walked along."

Belonging to a Catholic school usually meant going to mass one day during the week with my classmates, attending catechism on Saturdays, and then Sunday school and mass on Sundays.

There was one Sunday when we did not go to Sunday school or mass. The nuns called the house.

"Mom, it's Sister Nancy calling," yelled my brother, who answered the phone. Mom took the phone receiver from my brother.

"Yes," said Mom. One could only imagine what Sister Nancy was saying to Mom.

After a minute or two, Mom replied, "I am not feeling well. There is no one else to take these children to church. These are my children, and I will do what I want with them." Mom slammed the phone receiver down.

"None of you will be attending Catholic school next year. I am transferring you all to public school. There will be no more catechism, Sunday school, or mass. I do not ever want to hear the name of God or Jesus spoken in this house ever again."

Mom meant what she said. That was the last year we had anything to do with the Catholic church. Mom transferred us all to public school, except my oldest brother, who was attending seminary high school.

. . .

I remember Mom tried to make our summers enjoyable by going camping at least once a month in a pop-up trailer. We had so much fun studying nature, playing with ducks and ducklings, and enjoying God's world.

We got permission to take some ducklings home from one

of our favorite campsites. We raised those ducks in our backyard. We placed a plastic kid's pool in the ground with corner steps for the ducklings to play in the water and drink. They brought so much joy to all of us. When two of our ducks flew out of the yard, the police showed up at our door.

"There are two ducks flying around the neighborhood. We have been told they belong to you. Is that correct?"

Mom replied, "Yes, is there a problem? Have they done any damage? They always come home."

"No damage. However, according to the City Ordinances, ducks are banned in the city limits. You will need to get rid of them."

We rounded them up, including the ducklings, and took them to a local hospital which had several mini lakes on the grounds with lots of ducks, and released them. I remember all of us crying as we drove home.

. . .

One of our summer trips was to the Great Smoky Mountains on our way to Maine. The longest road trip was across America to Disneyland. Disney World did not exist when I was a child.

We rented a motorhome that broke down in Arizona. The heat was excruciating, well over 100 degrees, and we spent two days there before we moved on. We did make it to Disneyland and Knott's Berry Farm but were unable to go to Yosemite National Park due to the time spent in Arizona because of the breakdown.

My older brother was still around and did some driving, which meant all this happened when I was nine or ten years old. The last time we took a trip with the pop-up trailer, we had a jack-knife accident, and the trailer was damaged beyond repair.

Then, the family started falling apart.

Mom found out about some of the abuse, went into

third-degree interrogation mode, and was not able to process this in a responsible way. Family members were hurt physically and emotionally. Since she grew up in an abusive household, she managed it the same way it was handled when she was growing up. It took me a long time to understand that and to forgive her for the damage done.

. . .

My older brother left home after seminary high school, got married, and was living with his wife and stepdaughter.

The next oldest brother had all his belongings thrown out in the front yard while he was in the bathroom and told never to come back.

My oldest sister ran away from home one night while Mom was sleeping. Mom woke up the next morning and the remaining siblings had to tell Mom she ran away. Mom was uncontrollably angry at us for not waking her up to stop it.

My other sister got into a fight with Mom, and both were hurting each other, including strangling, scratching, and other physical harm. Someone called the police, and social services removed my sister from the home. She was placed with my brother to live. This all happened before I was twelve years old.

Before this sister was removed from the home, I remember she was part of the choir singing a school production of "Godspell." One of those songs has stuck in my mind for years. Whenever I become extremely emotional, depressed, or hopeless, I mutter the lyrics, "Oh dear Lord, three things I pray—to see thee more clearly, love thee more dearly, follow thee more nearly, day by day." Sometimes, these lyrics play in my mind like a broken record because I'm not sure of the exact things to pray for. However, they provide healing and balm to my broken spirit. Romans 8:26 (NIV) declares, "In the same way, the Spirit helps us in our weakness. We do not know what we ought to pray for, but the Spirit himself intercedes for us through wordless groans."

The only two children living in the home after this were my brother and me. It all happened so fast, and just like that, the family was split up. My large family became very small. Then, once again, when my brother turned eighteen, Mom threw him out of the house and then it was just myself and Mom in the house.

Back then, we did not have cell phones; the only landline phones in the house were in the family room and my mother's bedroom. Therefore, there were many years of no communication between my brother and me and our family members because Mom was always present. After Catholic school, Mom stopped working and did not work away from the home. If Mom were in her room and she heard us on the phone in the family room, she would pick up the receiver in her room and listen to the conversation. Therefore, no one called out and no one called in.

Communication with the other family members did not get much better after that. I do remember my two sisters inviting me to their weddings, which I attended; however, things were seriously strained as I had not been in their lives, and they had not been in my life since before I became a teenager. When I graduated high school, I went away to college for four years, moved to California immediately after college, and lived in California for four years.

As I write this, all family members have moved away from Miami. We have cordial communications, but everyone has their own lives, and there are hardly any physical get-togethers among siblings.

CHAPTER TWO–
THE AWKWARD YEARS

ADOPTED PARENTS

When my father died, making ends meet was extremely difficult for Mom. She had six children under the age of eight. With all of us, working a normal job wasn't going to work. Mom got a part-time job working in the cafeteria of the Catholic school we attended. We got lots of food during the day at a reduced price. Mom's household view was, everyone had to do their part to make money and help pay the bills.

A neighbor's family booked my older sister for a babysitting job with their family, and then a second family booked my other sister for babysitting with their family. There was a third family in the neighborhood also looking for a babysitter at the same time, and they thought I could help out. I was twelve years old and felt ready to "do my part" for the family. The family that wanted me to babysit lived in a kitty-corner lot to our house on a different street. Mrs. Stephens was the mother of the family, and she contacted me for the "initial interview." Mrs. Stephens and her husband had three adopted children, six, four, and one year old, and I was excited to meet the children and start my "working" life.

Mrs. Stephens stated, "We would need you to babysit during the summer. We are members of the country club, and we would like you to be able to take the children to the pool. Do you know how to swim?

"Yes."

"You could teach them to swim. Does this seem like something you would be interested in doing?"

"Yeah."

"We'd also need a babysitter on the weekends as we go out a lot. Would you be available given your school homework?"

"Definitely."

I was so excited that I would be able to make some money

and help with the household expenses. I thought Mom would love me more. To make this official, Mr. Stephens asked if he could meet Mom to introduce himself and answer any of Mom's questions regarding the babysitting position. It also was a wonderful opportunity for him to meet the other part of the family.

Mom met with Mr. Stephens and agreed that I could start babysitting and we'd see how it went before she agreed to the daily summer event. She eventually agreed to the daily summer event.

Ecclesiastes 9:11 (NIV) states, "I have seen something else under the sun: The race is not to the swift or the battle to the strong, nor does food come to the wise or wealth to the brilliant or favor to the learned, but time and chance happen to them all." This was my time and my chance to see God's blessings that lasted a lifetime.

Mr. and Mrs. Stephens were a Christian family, and I loved them. They were very perceptive and, over time, comprehended that I needed help. They could hear screaming and crying at my house because our backyards met. There were no air conditioning units to drown out the sounds because air conditioning was a luxury we could not afford. It became clear to the Stephens family what was going on at my home.

At times, the phone would ring, and I was usually the one who answered the phone.

"This is Mrs. Stephens. Is Judy there?"

"Hi, Mrs. Stephens. This is Judy speaking."

"Would you be able to babysit for a while right now? I have some chores and deadlines I need to complete."

"Let me ask Mom."

Putting my hand over the mouthpiece of the green, rotary dial phone, I asked, "Mom, Mrs. Stephens would like me to babysit now. May I go over?"

"How long will it be for?" asked Mom.

"Mrs. Stephens, Mom would like to know how long this will be for?"

"About three to four hours," replied Mrs. Stephens.

"Mom, Mrs. Stephens says about three to four hours. May I go?"

"Yes, but just remember you will still have to do your chores when you get home," emphasized Mom.

"Mrs. Stephens, Mom said yes, and I will be over shortly."

Mom rarely said no because it meant I was getting paid. She also knew that I was a straight-A student and always did my homework. I'd go over to Mrs. Stephens' house, and when I got there, she would ask me to play with the children. Over time, it became clear that she was not really going out. She just wanted me out of my house, and it became a common occurrence. The Stephens family knew if I was at their house, I wasn't being abused at home. But they always made sure to send me home with my hourly pay and a tip to make sure that they could continue to help however they could.

When I got home, I had to write in a book how much I made and how much was for the house expenses. I used one-half of my pay for family expenses.

. . .

When I was fifteen years old, through my high school grad-uation at seventeen years old, I had a part-time job after school until 6:00 every night. I would bike home, eat dinner, and sometimes I needed to go babysitting. If I was babysitting that night, I would do my homework after the children went to bed.

. . .

When I was sixteen years old, Mr. and Mrs. Stephens asked Mom if I could go to Eleuthera Island in the Bahamas for two weeks. They had a house there and would need me to babysit while they went out at night. Mom did not want me to go, but Mr. and Mrs. Stephens and I prayed that God would convince her. Mom finally said yes.

The Stephens' house was right on the ocean, and every night before bed, I would go for a walk on the beach. I had such great conversations with God, praying for love and peace in my life. Even though I was not going to church anymore, I still knew God was there and believed He would help me.

After our return from the Bahamas, Mr. and Mrs. Stephens introduced me to their church and asked me if I wanted to go to church with them on Sundays. I asked Mom, and she agreed, as long as it didn't interfere with my chores and schoolwork. There, I was introduced to the love of Jesus Christ and what he did for me on the cross. I approached Mom about joining their church.

"Mom, I would like to join Mr. and Mrs. Stephens' church. May I do that?"

"No. When you're an adult, you can join whatever church you want to join." And that was the end of that conversation. I was seventeen years old when this occurred.

When I was in high school, Mr. and Mrs. Stephens helped me choose four colleges to apply to and walked me through the process of completing the college applications. I applied and was accepted by two of the four colleges. The Stephens family helped me decide which one to accept.

All this discussion about college and leaving home did not make Mom happy. Mom believed as long as there was no money for college, she didn't have to worry about being alone and having to take care of herself without her "servant." However, I was turning eighteen years old, and Mom didn't have a say in that part of my future.

Mr. and Mrs. Stephen knew I could not afford college and told me they would pay for my entire college education:

room and board, tuition, books, meals, and everything else. Mrs. Stephens even insisted I join a sorority. Mrs. Stephens believed sorority life would help with my social skills and confidence. I went through Sorority Rush, pledged to a sorority, and became a little sister to a fraternity.

If that wasn't enough, every summer when I came home, Mr. Stephens helped me get a job at different law firms because he knew I wanted to be a lawyer. I was offered permanent jobs with a couple of these firms; however, I had to politely decline because we knew I needed to complete my education.

True to their word, Mr. and Mrs. Stephens paid for all my college years, and I graduated early with my bachelor's degree.

During my last semester at college, I interviewed for and accepted a great job in California for an electronics and defense company and believed I was now able to stand on my own two feet.

The love that Mr. and Mrs. Stephens showed me was the beginning of my understanding of what it means to be adopted by God, the ultimate loving parent. Romans 8:15 (NLT) says, "So you have not received a spirit that makes you fearful slaves. Instead, you received God's Spirit when he adopted you as his own children. Now we call him, 'Abba, Father.'"

ELEMENTARY SCHOOL/ HIGH SCHOOL

After Mom pulled us out of the Catholic school, I started attending fifth grade in the public school system with my brother. Mom had kept him back a year earlier in his education, and he and I were now in the same grade. This was all new to both of us, and we did not know any of the other students. Everyone at the school thought we were twins, and my brother and I did not see the need to correct them. We took the school bus and stuck together as much as possible, even though we did not have any classes together.

I remember trying to mind my own business, avoid trouble, get good grades to avoid Mom's punishment for bad grades, and just make it through the day.

One day, my science class had gone to lunch. On the way back from lunch, our science teacher lined us up along the wall before reentering the classroom. There were some children talking, which was a major no-no.

"There's to be no talking," said the science teacher.

Some of the children did not care and kept talking.

"One by one, you will enter the classroom, and everyone is going to be paddled because of the talking."

"But why should the ones who were not talking get paddled? Why don't you just paddle the ones who were talking?" asked one of the students.

"Because it was the class's responsibility to make sure your fellow classmates stopped talking and you did not do that. Now let's get started."

One by one, we entered the classroom, and the teacher paddled every one of us. Then, to make matters worse, a note was sent home to each parent stating, "Your child was paddled today

31

due to disobedience in the classroom. Please sign this note and have your child return it to the teacher tomorrow."

How was I going to explain to Mom that I was not the one talking and that everyone was paddled? I did not even want to think of the consequences of having her see and sign this note.

I did not experience any negative consequences because there was a child in the class with a physical disability that the teacher didn't know about when he paddled this student. The student's parents contacted the principal, and the teacher got into trouble for paddling the whole class, and the parents were notified. Finally, justification and vindication for telling Mom that I was not part of the disobedient students.

Things went along okay until one day on the playground, this mean boy I knew from my neighborhood came up to me and grabbed a part of my body in an inappropriate way.

By this age, I had finally learned that a lot of the sexual abuse and physical abuse that had been going on in my family and in the neighborhood was wrong.

One day, Mom got mad at me and said, "You should have known it was wrong, and how could you have let these things happen to you?"

"Mom, how was I supposed to know? You did not tell me that until you found out it had happened."

"I thought your older brothers and sisters had discussed these things with you."

"Well, they didn't!"

After this neighborhood boy had grabbed me, I ran him down and started choking him on the playground. I wanted him to die. My brother was on the playground that day, and he raced over and pulled me off this neighborhood kid. Too late! The playground monitors came over and took me to the principal's office, and they called Mom.

"Your child has been in a fight on the playground with a young boy. You will need to pick up your children from the principal's office."

Now I was really in trouble. Mom showed up at the principal's office to take us home.

Mom waited until we got into the car to ask, "Why did you try to choke that boy on the playground?"

"Mom, he grabbed me and hurt me."

Turning to my brother, Mom asked, "Did you see this?"

"Yes, Mom, he grabbed her in a bad place, and she tried to choke him. I tried to race over and get her off as quickly as possible, but I was on the other side of the playground when I saw it."

"Okay, well, don't let it happen again."

"Yes, Mom."

I did not get punished that day.

. . .

For summer fun, we lived really close to a natural coral rock formation public swimming pool. Everyone in the family went to the pool daily for swimming lessons in the morning. After swimming lessons, we would go home and do our chores. If we finished early enough, we would get permission to go back to the swimming pool for fun. Mom liked the swimming pool because it was close enough for us to walk there, there were numerous lifeguards on duty, and it would give her some peace and quiet at home.

One day at the swimming pool, when I was a teenager, one of the boys came up to me and grabbed me inappropriately. I raced after him in the water, caught up with him, and tried to drown him in the swimming pool. Again, I believe God had placed my brother nearby, who saw what happened, and he got me off the boy before the lifeguards could see this and throw me out of the pool. If you got thrown out of the pool, you could not come back, and I could not explain that to Mom.

My anger against people for sexually abusing me was uncontrollable. I did not know how to process the shame and condemnation that I felt. Anytime the discussion of prior past abuse came up, Mom would say things that made me feel as if I had done something to deserve it or should have been able to stop it, even though it had started when I was five years old and continued on for several years.

. . .

Somewhere during my tender years, I developed another personality that helped me deal with all the sexual and physical abuse. Her name was "Shaggy," and she was my best friend. When something bad was happening, sweet, loving Shaggy would appear, and I would hide my face behind my long blonde hair. Shaggy was this cute little dog. Everyone loves dogs, and no one hurts dogs, right? People loved Shaggy as she was fun and friendly, and no one ever tried to hurt her.

When I went to junior high school, during the first year of school integration in my city, I met this wonderful friend. She called me "Nut" because she thought I was crazy and did not like my nickname Shaggy, and her nickname was "Sweet Pea." Together we went through junior and senior high school inseparable. The only time we could spend together was at school because Mom did not allow any of us to go over to other people's houses or have them come over to our house because of the history of visitors in the house.

Sweet Pea, being much taller than me and more like my big sister, protected me any time a boy would come close and bother me. We had several classes together, and we helped each other with assignments and homework at school.

One day in high school, this girl I did not know came up to me and said, "Hi, I'm Michael's girlfriend." She was referring to one of my next-door neighbors who was part of the sexual abuse going on in my house whenever he and his brother came over. They no longer lived next to us as social services had told them to move for their own protection after the police arrested the father for trying to kill one of the sons with a machete.

"So?" I asked.

"He told me all about the things he used to do to you and how much he enjoyed it."

I walked away. What response would anyone have to a statement like that? I thought that I had finally gotten away from the abuse and the abusers, and here I was being reminded of it through a total stranger. Why would she approach me? What joy did she get out of approaching me and telling me those things? Was she going to tell everyone in school? All I wanted to do was hide.

To deal with the situation, Shaggy ("Nut") appeared, and I found Sweet Pea, told her what happened, and she told me she would protect me. Sweet Pea and I had spent hours talking about our childhoods, and she knew all about mine. I knew I could trust her to keep it silent.

The extent to which Shaggy protected me included when I moved to California after I graduated from college. My license plate in California was "Shaggy1." She was the best because Judy was not. I felt so condemned, and I had not yet learned how much God loved me. I did not understand Romans 8:1 (NLT), "So now there is no condemnation for those who belong to Christ Jesus." I did not know what it meant to belong to Christ Jesus.

CHAPTER THREE–
THE DETERMINED YEARS

FLORIDA STATE UNIVERSITY

I have read the story of the prodigal [daughter] numerous times, and I'm here to tell you I am not the prodigal [daughter]. Worse! I am the older [sister] who stayed home taking care of the land and the [mother] while the prodigal [siblings] were out enjoying life, spending lots of money, with no care in the world.

Growing up at home, I was not allowed to have any friends over, nor was I allowed to go to anyone else's home unless Mom was with me, which rarely happened. I was not allowed to go into neighbors' houses without Mom being present. I'm sure this is because of all of the sexual problems with neighbors growing up. Anyway, back in the '60s and '70s, most parents wanted their children outside playing. We did not have cell phones, cable TV, streaming networks, or any of that. We had one black-and-white TV, and you could only watch TV on special occasions and when all your chores were done. Once I finished my chores on Saturdays, all I wanted to do was to get out of the house and find some neighborhood friends to play with. We usually ended up at the golf course around the block. When Mom blew her whistle, we ran home as fast as we could. We always had to be home before sunset, no matter what! I did get permission to go to prom and grad night; however, these were the only social events of my childhood.

After all the family members had left home, gotten kicked out, run away from home, or removed by Social Services, the only siblings left at home to endure Mom's inability to cope were my youngest male sibling and me. All I could ask was how my siblings could leave like that and leave the two of us here alone with Mom.

Didn't they even care what was going to happen to us? Didn't they realize that Mom was going to take her anger out on us because of what they had done? It was only a matter of time before my brother was forced to leave the home and live in his car like some of the other siblings, and now, I was all alone with Mom.

Then I went off to Florida State University and became a prodigal [daughter]. Riotous living. Rebellion. Live and let live. Do whatever.

I was a social infant and outcast when I arrived at Florida State University in August of 1977, set up in an all-girls dormitory with a sophomore roommate. Back then, dorm rooms were basic, with a bed, a chest of drawers, and a small table. There were no private bathrooms or showers. This was a new, terrifying experience for me.

I signed up for Sorority Rush, a two-week-long event before classes started. This was where students had the opportunity to go through all the sororities' parties and decide if they wanted to join one of them. I promised my adoptive parents that I would do that because they thought it would pull me out of my shell. I chose a sorority and began my pledge period. The sorority had parties all the time with different fraternities, and then there were events for all the sororities and fraternities. I ended up becoming a "Little Sister" to a fraternity which meant that when the fraternity had its parties, the Little Sisters would attend the parties and assist the men.

As a pledge to a sorority, there were certain responsibilities like attending all mandatory functions, maintaining a certain GPA, learning proper etiquette, setting up place settings for formal meals, and other social skills I never learned at home. I did learn some of these skills when I was babysitting for my adoptive family because they were always entertaining. They would have me there for all the parties, and I would watch the children and help set up; however, it was not as formal as the sorority house.

There were many rewards of being part of a sorority, including being able to have informal breakfast and lunch meals and formal dining meals at the sorority house. I preferred the good cooking at the sorority house and tried to have all of my meals there. The chef was friendly, and her food was excellent. I was beginning to come out of my social cocoon.

When I lived at home, all I did was go to school, work, babysit, and my brother and I split the chores in the house. Now that I was "free," I went wild. It seemed like I drank alcohol every night. I started smoking cigarettes, going to all kinds of clubs with sorority sisters and fraternity brothers, and "experiencing the world," something I never did when I lived at home.

When I came home from college during recess and summer breaks, Mom and I continued to fight about everything. She thought I dressed like a street walker, wanted to know where my "values" went, and she did not like who I was becoming.

I told her, "I took all the values you beat into me, evaluated them for my life, and got rid of the ones that weren't going to work in my life."

Secretly, I did not want her to know how miserable I was. The summer before my first year at college, my adoptive parents gave me a purebred Beagle puppy. Butch was full of unconditional love, and I thought he would make a good companion for my mom while I was away at college. She agreed I could keep Butch.

I arrived home from college for Thanksgiving break my freshman year and was met at the door by Mom and Butch.

"You must get rid of Butch tonight if you plan to stay here. I want him out of the house now. You can use the car, but you get rid of him now."

Another victim was kicked out of her house.

I had nowhere to stay, so I put the leash on Butch and got in the car hysterically crying. I started driving north because I knew the pound was in the north end of town. I did not want him to go to the pound because I was afraid they would kill him. Butch had no idea what was going on. When I arrived at the pound, it was closed, and I did not know what to do. I was at the gate crying when the security guard approached.

"What's wrong?"

"My mom is making me give up my puppy, or else I can't return home."

I was surprised the guard understood what I was saying as I was crying so hard.

"Is he house-trained?"

"Yes."

"Calm down. The pound is closed, and you cannot leave him here; however, my family and I are looking for a puppy, and I will take him from you."

"Really?"

"Yes, my family will adore him and give him lots of love."

"Bye, Butch."

I walked away believing this was God's hand, and I had peace leaving Butch with him.

. . .

At the end of my freshman year, I was voted in as the Treasurer of the sorority and that gave me a private room because I had to have a locked closet and private area to work on the financial books of the sorority. I loved the sisterhood I felt at the sorority and got extremely close to several sisters. I spent time with one of the sisters at her parent's home just outside of Tallahassee during some weekends. It was wonderful to experience life in someone else's family.

As an adult, during one of my summers when I came home from college, I spent time together with my brother and his friends. We would go drinking and clubbing and then hang out at our friends' homes. One night, I ended up in another sexual encounter that I could not get away from, and when it was over, I went downstairs and called Mom. It was almost 1:00 a.m. in the morning, and I did not know where my brother was in the house. However, I knew I had to get out of the house.

"Mom, will you come pick me up? I'll be heading north walking down Alhambra Circle toward home."

"Yes, I'll be there shortly."

I saw Mom drive past me heading south. She turned the seven-passenger station wagon around and pulled over on the side of the road. I got in the passenger seat of the car.

"Are you okay?"

"I'm fine. I'm tired and I wanted to come home, and I couldn't find anyone to drive me home. I figured you didn't want me walking home alone. Thank you for picking me up."

Mom and I never discussed that night, but she knew something had happened based on my disheveled look and my tears. I appreciated her for not pushing the issue with me. My brother never knew about the issue. All he knew was that something had happened because I never wanted to go out with him and that friend ever again.

Back at college, the emotional attachments at the sorority house grew stronger after the horrible sexual encounters I experienced as a child and now as an adult, and I didn't want to spend any time with men. I became involved with one of the sisters; however, no matter how hard I tried to get her to love me, she was in love with another sorority sister. Having been abused by men and now rejected by women I thought cared about me, I tried to kill myself by taking an overdose of narcotic medication I had. One of my sisters found me and immediately took me to the hospital, where they pumped my stomach, kept me overnight, and turned me in to the authorities. Apparently, it was against the law in Florida to attempt to commit suicide.

Before I could leave the hospital, I had to deal with the authorities. I was given an option. Go straight to jail, destroy my college education, or try and get my life in order by going to mandatory therapy for six months. I chose mandatory therapy.

I went to therapy every week for six months. In the beginning,

I felt like I knew what I could say to the therapist, and then they would say I was "cured," and I could stop going to therapy.

However, at some point during this therapy, I also started going to a non-denominational church, trying to find this "God" who had been banned from my childhood. God, to me, was foreign during my childhood. As part of the Catholic church, they would talk about God; however, all your spiritual communications were done with nuns or priests during confessions, and then saying "Hail Marys" as penitence for sins. God was not part of my childhood. Then, as a teenager, my adoptive family introduced me to God and Jesus Christ as part of their church; however, Mom would not let me join, and I could not go with them sometimes. It seemed like a nice story about God loving everyone and Jesus dying for everyone; however, it was all in my mind and had never made it to my heart.

God started opening my heart, and through honest communication with the therapist, I learned that I could overcome my emotional baggage with God's help. I just didn't know how to do that. I was trying to earn respect from God and everyone around me so they would love me, and I kept messing up, and nobody loved me. I learned that God loved me, and He had plans for my life, no matter what had happened in the past. I just had to believe it.

In Matthew 13, Jesus said, "As he scattered them across his field, some seeds fell on a footpath, and the birds came and ate them. Other seeds fell on shallow soil with underlying rock. The seeds sprouted quickly because the soil was shallow. But the plants soon wilted under the hot sun, and since they didn't have deep roots, they died. Other seeds fell among thorns that grew up and choked out the tender plants. Still other seeds fell on fertile soil, and they produced a crop that was thirty, sixty, and even a hundred times as much as had been planted! Anyone with ears to hear should listen and understand."

I had experienced all these seeds of God and Jesus during

my lifetime. The seeds that fell on the footpath during my childhood were the seeds of the Catholic church, but then the nuns and priests ate them. As I grew into my teens and twenties, the seeds fell on shallow soil with underlying rock, and they sprouted quickly, but the soil was too shallow. Anytime there was another trigger or emotional issue, these seeds did not have deep roots, and they died. Then the seeds fell among thorns, and life's worries choked out the tender plants.

It was only recently that I learned that no matter whether we are the prodigal [siblings] or the elder one who stayed home, the Father who is waiting for our return, day in and day out, with loving patience and open arms, is our heavenly Father, God. I guess some of these seeds took root.

THE BUNDY YEARS

After Christmas break at college, everyone arrived back at school and began the winter session. On January 15, 1978, there was an announcement over the loudspeaker at my dorm at 6:00 a.m.

"All students, please report to the main lobby right away for a mandatory security briefing. Residential Assistants, knock on every door on your floor and have every resident quickly put on a bathrobe and make their way to the main lobby. Take notes of any residents who are not in their rooms and make a list to give to us when you arrive for the meeting."

Floor by floor, we all made our way to the main lobby, where there were residential counselors waiting for us.

"Good morning, all. We apologize for the early morning briefing; however, we must discuss university security. Earlier this morning, there was a vicious attack at one of the sorority houses off campus, and some sorority sisters were killed and others injured. We do not know all of the details right now; however, the attacker is on the loose and has not been captured. No one will be allowed to walk on or near campus alone. Security is in the process of being tightened and we are adding more security officers as we speak. There will be buses providing transportation throughout the campus. Maps will be provided with the stops and the routes."

I was in shock. What sorority house? Why won't they tell us more details? The briefing went on for what seemed like forever. All I wanted to do was to get dressed and run over to my sorority house to make sure everyone was okay. Back then, we did not have cell phones. There were only pay phones in the dormitory, and I knew that every pay phone would be busy with residents calling parents to let them know they were okay or calling others to find out if they were okay. I looked around the room to see if there were any other pledges from my sorority that I could get to walk over to the sorority house to find out about our sorority. I saw two and made my way over to them.

SEEING THE HAND OF GOD

"Can you guys get dressed and head over to the sorority house now to make sure it wasn't our sorority house?"

"Yes, absolutely."

"Let's meet back here in ten minutes after the briefing concludes."

"Okay."

The briefing ended, and I ran back to my room, got dressed, and met my fellow pledges in the main lobby. We were so concerned we ran part of the way and quickly walked the other part of the way. We did not live close to the sorority house as it was all the way across campus. When we arrived at the sorority house and knocked on the door, all the women were there in the living room, just finishing a security briefing of their own.

"Good morning, pledges. We are all safe here. It was not our sorority house; however, it was the Chi Omega sorority house. As we just discussed with the sisters, no one will be allowed to walk anywhere alone. We will be hiring a full-time security guard who will assist the House Mother with our safety. All doors must be kept locked at all times. You will not be allowed to prop open doors, even the one leading to the parking lot. As we have some empty rooms and beds in the sorority house, if you feel like you would be safer living at the sorority house, we can take in a few of you. If we are having a late function and you do not want to go back to your dorm room for the night, we have empty bunk beds upstairs and day cots in the rooms to accommodate anyone who wishes to stay here."

At the sorority house, I was able to call home and let Mom and my adoptive family know that I was safe and that I would be spending more time at the sorority house, given the security situation at the University. I did not want them to worry.

I was not having an enjoyable time with my sophomore dormitory roommate. She was helping herself to all my stuff, including makeup, clothes, and food, and sneaking her boyfriend into the all-women's dorm room at night. I would come home from class, and the door would be locked from the inside. I would knock, and she would open the door slightly and tell me that she had company and I had to find another place to sleep that night. If that wasn't the worst, she was using my bed with him. I was disgusted. There were several nights that I slept on the floor of another resident. It appeared there was nothing I could do as the Resident Assistant was friends with her. The Resident Assistant and my roommate had been on the floor together when my roommate was a freshman the year before. The Resident Assistant knew what was going on but looked the other way. There were mornings when you could hear women screaming in the bathroom because they walked in there to go to the bathroom or to take a shower, and there was a man in the all-women's dormitory. Everyone just kept quiet about it.

Now that the sorority was offering up vacant rooms and beds, I eventually ended up spending most of my nights at the sorority house during my freshman year after the Chi Omega incident.

About a month later, serial killer Ted Bundy was caught. Over time, the full details of his time in Tallahassee were revealed little by little. I realized God was watching over me the whole time I was at Tallahassee, however, especially the night that Bundy went on his killing spree.

On January 14, 1978, I had gone to a fraternity party on "fraternity row." I got myself into a compromising sexual situation, which I could not physically get out of. When the event was over, I was emotionally distraught, quickly dressed, ran out of the fraternity house, and headed back to my sorority house, which was on the next block. I wanted to spend some time with my sorority sisters before I headed home to the dorm room. I knew I was not going to tell them what happened because I was ashamed and felt dirty. I just wanted to be among friends and try and deal with this situation on my own. After spending some time at the sorority house, I then walked home alone. This was just one event in college that left me emotionally scarred. I tried to rationalize everything that happened, saying it did not matter because I was already damaged goods before I went to college, and this was just more damage.

During the next several weeks, I was having bad dreams about the sexual encounter and the fears of Bundy still being on the street while sleeping at the sorority house in one of the bunk beds. I was sleeping in the top bunk and fell out of the bed, landing hard on the floor. I immediately went to the bathroom and realized I was bleeding. To this day, I do not know if I was pregnant; however, on several of my subsequent gynecological exams, the doctors asked me if I had ever been pregnant because of the size of my uterus. I told them no.

Little did I know that Bundy was living in the boarding house right across the street from the fraternity house where I had been attending the party. I had walked to the sorority house alone and walked back to the dorm alone the night that Bundy was out looking for his next victim(s). Thank You, God, it was not me. I subsequently learned that two of the Chi Omega sisters who were attacked had spent time with me during the Sorority Rush, trying to convince me to join their sorority.

CHAPTER FOUR–
THE LOST YEARS

YOUNG & DUMB AND
SEARCHING FOR WISDOM

I start this chapter by acknowledging God's Word in Proverbs 29:18 (AMP), "Where there is no vision [no revelation of God and His word], the people are unrestrained; But happy and blessed is he who keeps the law [of God]."

California was more of a wilderness in my life, full of unrestrained living, including being sexually active with several different men. I learned that not only was this against God's will for my life, but all these men were not good for me and my future. I had just come out of a two-year relationship with a man that I lived with and who I allowed to manipulate me because I did not have the confidence or self-esteem to stand on my own. The ex-boyfriend had told me to leave, and I ended up moving into a house that represented the comedy show *Three's Company*. There were two females, one male, and the male's girlfriend, who did not really live there; however, she spent a lot of time at the house. I wish I could say that the guy and us girls kept to ourselves; however, that would be a lie.

One day at work, one of my co-workers approached me because she knew my situation. We always had lunch together.

"I would like you to meet my son. He also works here but in a different department. I think you would hit it off."

"Sure, I'd like to meet him."

I met him, and we hit it off. I eventually moved into his house with his mother and father, his sister, and her boyfriend. There were six of us in the home, and it was like being part of a family that I lost many years before.

My boyfriend did a lot of marijuana. No one in the family said anything negative about it if he was able to maintain himself, hold down his job, and help with the family.

It was through this boyfriend and his sister that I got involved in illegal drug activities. My boyfriend's sister was the dealer. I spent most of my paychecks buying drugs. My boyfriend was more involved in other drugs than I was, and the cocktails he created were making him a wreck. He was high all the time at work, and his mother and father never knew or refused to see it.

One day, my boyfriend, his sister, her boyfriend, and I went up into the mountains for a hike, do drugs, and enjoy the day. When we came back for dinner, my boyfriend was so high he could barely stand in the kitchen while dishing up his meal. We told his parents that we were not feeling well and that we would be eating our meal in his room. I will never forget how sick he was that night. It was then that I decided it was time for me to move away from Los Angeles and this negative lifestyle. It was going nowhere good.

I applied for a position in Sunnyvale with a subsidiary of my current company I was working for. I got the job and subsequently left Southern California and moved to Northern California. I left a lot of my belongings in a backyard shed with this young man and his family until I could get situated in Northern California. I told them I would be back to pick this stuff up when situated.

I remember calling about a month or two after being in Northern California to arrange to pick up my stuff. By then, I was married, and Theo was going with me to retrieve my personal belongings. The mom told me that after I left, this young man had serious mental issues and was hospitalized. His mom blamed me for her son's condition, believing I was the one who introduced him to drugs. They never knew that it was he and his sister who introduced me to the drugs. I had never done them before dating him. After I had picked up my belongings, I told Theo that I wanted to go by the bank where I knew his sister worked, because I wanted some more information on what happened. When I left Los Angeles, this mom was cordial to me; however, now she was belligerent to me, and I wanted to know why.

I entered the bank and went to the teller where she was.

"What happened to Peter?" I asked as quietly as possible, understanding this was her place of work.

"Let me take a break. I'll meet you in the parking lot of the bank, and we can discuss it."

Within a couple of minutes, she appears in the parking lot.

"Your mom is accusing me of getting him on these hard drugs and blaming me for his current condition. What happened?"

"He ended up overdosing and nearly died. When he came to, he was emotionally unstable, and they thought it best to put him into a mental hospital to get well."

"Did you tell your mom that you were doing the drugs first with your boyfriend and that you were the dealer for your brother and me? Did you tell them that I did not even know about these drugs before meeting you?"

"Of course not. Please, no matter what happens, you cannot tell my mom anything about me being the dealer or introducing you to these drugs. I'm begging you."

"I'll think about it."

I left that parking lot, and that was the last time I spoke to anyone in that family.

My life was continuing its pattern of getting into bad situations, walking away, and never returning to speak to anyone again. I did it with home, my family, college, with each relationship in California. I did not know how to deal with these situations, and walking away was my only solution.

. . .

I knew that to start healing, I would have to learn how to forgive others for what they had done to me, as well as forgive myself for all the "wrongs" I had done to others and myself. Romans

12:19 (NLT) provided the foundation: "Dear friends, never take revenge. Leave that to the righteous anger of God. For the Scriptures say, 'I will take revenge; I will pay them back,' says the Lord." I am daily reminded to forgive others and myself, as Christ has forgiven my "sins." I am glad God has given me another chance today to let go of my hurt and anger and release them all to Him.

. . .

After leaving Northern California and returning to Miami, my spiritual life was non-existent. Despite the fact I was now married and supposed to be getting wiser, it seemed like I was floundering in everything I did. Theo and I both knew about God, knew about His Son, Jesus Christ, knew about the Bible and God's Word, but we did not have the wisdom to apply this knowledge to our everyday lives. I knew that Theo had occasionally gone to church in England with his ex-wife and children, and I had occasionally gone to church during college; however, we were not a united couple spiritually.

When I was twenty-nine years old, Theo surprised me one night, telling me that there were some missionaries coming over to visit that night. He knew I was searching for God and God's plan for our lives and did not quite know where to start. These missionaries had contacted him one day while I was at work, and he decided to hear what they had to say. I spent several months studying with these missionaries and decided I was ready to join the church. I was baptized and received the Holy Spirit on my thirtieth birthday, and it was one of the most joyous days of my life, next to giving birth to Annette. Theo was already well-versed in this church, and he was able to be a part of my baptism.

From that point on, my life changed dramatically. I would get up every morning at 5:30 a.m., have my coffee, and study God's Word before going to work. Theo was driving across the country for his work, and my housemate always slept in late, so I had the house to myself. I would go to church several times a week for women's activities and Sunday services. Then, I started having questions about the church I had joined and did not believe that I should continue to attend. I spoke with Theo about it, and we decided to join a church together, which we did. That church was the Evangelical Church that sent us to Liberia, West Africa, as missionaries.

I have watched God's Word radically transform my life day by day. Romans 12:2 AMP summarizes my transformation succinctly. "And do not be conformed to this world [any longer with its superficial values and customs], but be transformed and progressively changed [as you mature spiritually] by the renewing of your mind [focusing on godly values and ethical attitudes], so that you may prove [for yourselves] what the will of God is, that which is good and acceptable and perfect [in His plan and purpose for you]." This is a day-by-day occurrence; however, I know by the grace and mercy of Jesus Christ that He is transforming me, and I just need to walk in His plan.

When I talk with coworkers and friends now, they think that I have been a godly person my entire life. They are shocked to hear the road I have traveled to get to where I am now.

I know that God loves me, that Jesus died on the cross for my sins, that Jesus is my Savior, and God has a definite plan for my life, even at this age. One of my favorite scriptures is Jeremiah 29:11 (NLT), "For I know the plans I have for you, says the Lord. They are plans for good and not for disaster, to give you a future and a hope." I am now taking steps to walk in what I believe to be God's will for my life and follow His plans for good, to give me a future and a hope for Annette and me.

LOVE AT FIRST SIGHT...
'TIL DEATH DO US PART

After moving to Northern California to get away from the drug-fueled, harmful relationships I had been involved in, I went to work for a high-tech, high-security company requiring at least a secret and/or top-secret security clearance. Guess what! All of my co-workers were snorting drugs, and within days of starting work, I had access to whatever I wanted, and the vicious cycle began again. The women would all go to the bathroom at the same time, and the little bottles of drugs were being passed under the stalls. It was crazy! I was attempting to transfer my Top-Secret security clearance from the Southern California company to the Northern California company.

Sitting on my fold-out, foam rubber couch/sofa in my studio apartment, I cried to myself, "I am so lonely!"

The move from Southern California to Northern California was traumatic. I had just broken up with a short-term boyfriend, and it was not a friendly breakup.

I had met some acquaintances at work; however, I was not sure where that would end up.

"Come out with us after work," yelled Becky as we walked to the parking lot.

"You have to get out, otherwise you'll just keep staying depressed."

"Fine, I'll go out one night so you will stop bugging me," I replied. I really wanted to get to know the area, but I was scared and emotionally hurt, and I played it off as if I did not care. "I'll follow you," was my final reply as we reached our cars, which were side-by-side in the parking lot.

"Great, it's not that far away. Just stay close."

My silver Toyota Celica followed Becky's red Toyota Camry.

After about fifteen minutes of left turns and right turns and lots of lights in between, we pulled into a shopping center. Reluctantly, I exited my vehicle slowly.

"Come on, hurry up, this is our neighborhood hang-out," exclaimed Becky, pointing to a plain-looking, store-front bar called The Raven. "Everyone is already here."

I walked in and looked around. It was a little bar with a few tables and chairs around a small dance floor, two pool tables in the back, and dartboards. There were about ten to fifteen people in the bar.

I wanted to turn around and leave and go home when an older gentleman with dark brown hair, dark brown eyes, and a mustache walked up to me.

"Would you like to dance?"

I really did not want to be there and hadn't even had a chance to get my bearings in this place when I replied, "No, get lost."

"What was that all about?" asked Becky.

"Some guy wants me to dance."

"Oh, that's Theo. He is a regular here with all of us. He does not work where we work, but we all know him, and he's okay. He works at some paint factory or something like that," retorted Becky.

Becky and I moved to the back of the bar. I didn't want to dance, but I did want to play pool. I put my quarter on the table for the next game. I went to the bar while waiting for my turn to play. "Jack and Coke, please." I played several games of pool.

I watched as my co-workers interacted with Theo, how he carried himself, how he played darts, and how much fun they were all having. I felt bad about how I handled myself earlier and walked over to where everyone was.

Remorsefully, I walked over to Theo and said, "I'm sorry for being so rude earlier. I've just arrived in Sunnyvale, and this was my first night out. I really did not want to come here, but Becky insisted. Do you still want to dance?"

"Sure," Theo said, reaching for my hand and escorting me to the dance floor.

I thought to myself, *Wow, this guy can really dance!*

We danced, played pool, played darts, talked, and laughed with everyone else until The Raven closed at 2:00 a.m. We all walked out together, and Theo escorted me to my car.

I couldn't believe we closed down the bar. "Wow, I don't know how I can be at work at 6:30 a.m., four and one-half hours from now, if I go home and sleep."

"Neither do I."

"Hey, would you like to come to my studio apartment? It's fairly close, and we can just hang out and talk."

"Sure, let's do it."

Theo followed me home and we climbed the stairs to my apartment.

We talked about life, family, jobs, God, anything and everything for the next four hours keeping each other awake, despite many yawns. We both had to leave at 6:00 a.m. to get to work on time.

As Theo was saying good morning to me, he asked, "Hey, Wednesday nights, I go to this lively Pentecostal church. Would you like to go on Wednesday?" asked Theo.

"Okay, what time and where?"

"I'll pick you up around 6:00 p.m."

"Great, have a good day at work, and get some sleep tonight."

"Same to you, bye."

I watched him walk to his fire-engine red Chevy Chevette. The back of his car looked full of stuff I could not make out in the dark of the night.

I went back into my apartment and got ready for work. As I got dressed, all I could think about was Theo and our discussions. I drove to work, clocked in, and saw one of my co-workers who immediately inquired about the night.

"So, how was your night? I saw you spent a lot of time with Theo after you started dancing with him. Then it looked like you left together."

"It was amazing. We have so much in common, and we understand each other. We're supposed to get together Wednesday night for church."

By the time Wednesday came around, neither Theo nor I were physically able to go to church, so we canceled that night and agreed to meet back up at the bar on Friday night.

Friday came around, and one of my co-workers stated, "We are going back to the bar tonight; would you like to join us?"

Even though I was exhausted, I said, "Sure, do you have any extra speed to get me through the day?"

"No problem, now let's get to work."

After work, we drove over to the bar. I walked in and saw Theo playing darts in the back room. He saw me and came over.

"Hi, did you finally get some sleep?"

"Yes, I did. Did you?"

"I sure did."

We started drinking, doing drugs, playing pool, and playing darts, and around 11:00 p.m., I had to go to the bathroom. When I came out of the bathroom, Theo called me over to the bar to sit down and talk.

"Judy, would you marry me?"

"What, is this a joke? What are you talking about?"

"I love it when we are together, and I can't stop thinking about you when I'm away from you. How do you feel about me?"

"I feel the same way, but I just do not know about this. Is this a game?"

"No, I really would like to marry you if you would have me."

"I'll have to think about it," then walked away and went over to one of my co-workers.

"Theo just asked me to marry him. Did you know anything about this?"

"No, what did you tell him?"

"That I'd have to think about it?"

"How do you feel about him? Do you like him? Are you considering this?"

"I do like him, but we just met. I'm going to call my mom and discuss it with her."

I entered the phone booth, sat down on the bench, and called Mom.

"Hi, Mom, were you sleeping?"

"No, you know I am up all hours of the night. What is up?"

"I met this man, and he wants me to marry him, and I wanted to get your advice."

"Well, I do not know why you are calling me since you always do whatever you want to do. If you do get married, I will not be there," and Mom hung up the phone.

I started crying because Mom was right. Since I left home, I did whatever I wanted to do. After I went away to college and came home during breaks, Mom and I would have verbal fights, and she would say, "Who the heck are you? I do not even know you anymore. Where are your values and morals?"

"I am your daughter, and I took 'your' values and morals and picked the ones that worked in my life and kept them and the ones that did not work in my life, I got rid of. This is me."

I came out of the phone booth and found one of my co-workers and tried to have fun while I wrestled with this ominous question. I was twenty-four years old, had been involved in several disastrous relationships, and honestly believed that this might be my only marriage proposal. Theo was good-looking, a gentleman, industrious, homeless, and fun to be around. We came from similar backgrounds and utterly understood each other's pains and insecurities.

After two hours of avoiding Theo while getting my thoughts together, I finally went back to Theo.

"Yes, I will marry you."

"Who did you call in the phone booth?"

"My mom."

"I saw you crying. Are you okay?"

"Yes, my mom and I had a verbal fight, and she basically shut me down."

"Well, would you like to elope to Nevada now to get married?"

"Are you serious?"

"Yes, what is stopping us?"

"Well, let me ask one of my co-workers if she would go with us to Nevada and stand up for me since I don't have anyone else?"

After getting one of my co-workers to go with me, I said to Theo, "Are you ready?"

We eloped to Reno, Nevada, and after our five-hour drive, we arrived at downtown Reno. I knew Theo did not have a ring for me, nor did I own a ring, so we found a jewelry store that was open. I purchased a gold, round etched ring, and we set off to find a wedding place. We found "The Hitching Post" and walked in.

"We'd like to get married," said Theo to the woman behind the counter.

"Is this going to be your wife?"

CHAPTER FOUR—THE LOST YEARS

"Yes."

"Who is this other person?"

"That is her friend from work—the witness."

Theo and I were married exactly one week and one day after we met. We drove back to Sunnyvale, California, and on Saturday night, we walked into The Raven, where all our friends were. Theo asked for everyone to come to the bar, as he had ordered drinks for everyone to celebrate our marriage.

"Judy and I are married, and we want to share our marriage with everyone."

"You're joking, right?"

"Nope," I said as I pulled out my marriage certificate.

I went back to work on Monday and went straight to my supervisor.

"I need to go to HR."

"Why, did you get married or something?"

"Yes, as a matter of fact, I did get married." I went to HR and changed my name. My official married life began.

The Raven was "our" place until we left California at the end of the year in 1984.

There were days when I knew that I was being followed, and the drug situation was getting extremely dangerous.

When we left California in 1984, that was the last time I used any drugs that were not physician-prescribed. I have been clean and sober since 1984.

. . .

When we arrived in Florida in 1984, we stayed with Mom until we could get on our feet. We arrived with nothing but the clothes and items we had in the van we drove from California

. . .

to Florida. The only thing Mom said about my marriage and my husband was, "You must have been desperate for a lay." How condescending! And yet, during the time we stayed with her, which was only a couple of months, she kept making statements about my husband like, "Wow, he's got nice gams." Was my mother hitting on my husband?

Theo and I immediately got jobs and started saving our money. Within a few months, we had moved out to a furnished one-bedroom apartment. We bought a broken-down car with rust holes all over, including the engine cover, from my brother for $100. Theo was a good mechanic, and when we were not working, we fixed up the car, including painting it with spray paint cans and putting designs on it to cover the bad areas. Theo had good ideas. We eventually traded in that car for $2,000 for a newer car and kept saving our money.

As a result of a terrible accident at the apartment building we were living at, Theo's back was injured, and he could not work for almost two years. We sued the apartment building for a negligent safety issue. All we wanted was enough money to pay Theo's medical bills and some of his lost wages. We received $16,000 ($20,000 less $4,000 for attorney's fees), paid off our medical bills, and were able to put a down payment on a three-bedroom, one-bath house that was being seller-financed. We lived in that house until Theo got his missionary post in Liberia, West Africa.

. . .

After five years and five days of being divorced from Theo, in December 2006, Theo asked me to remarry him. I did not hesitate to say yes because I still loved him. We went to the courthouse, got the marriage license, waited for the three-day waiting period to expire, and had my office manager remarry us.

Ten days later, Theo was feeling sick and having a tough time breathing, so we took him to the doctor. The doctors ran some tests, did some scans, and brought us back into the office to discuss the results.

The doctor stated, "We have found a suspicious-looking mass in your abdomen, and we would like to do a biopsy as soon as possible. It's quite large and appears to be pushing on your lungs, which is the reason for your breathing problems."

Theo replied, "How can I have a large mass in my abdomen? I have been coming to you yearly for a full exam for the last ten years. I told you that I have not been eating hardly anything lately and yet my stomach was getting bigger and bigger. How can this be?" There was no good response.

Theo was scheduled for an emergency biopsy, and they concluded the mass was malignant. Theo was referred to a surgeon for immediate surgery.

Theo went to four surgeons, including the Chief of Surgery at one of the most renowned hospitals in Miami. The reason for so many surgeons was they all told Theo and me to get his affairs in order, and he only had about three months to live. The massive tumor in his abdomen had attached itself to all his major organs and was so large it was crushing his lungs. I did some extensive research on the internet and found a local surgeon who had experience with this kind of tumor during his residency at one of the famous New York hospitals. We set up an emergency appointment.

The doctor looked at the films, test results, and us and said, "I think I can save your life if you have the surgery immediately. It will be a risky surgery and will take about five to six hours. Do you want me to schedule it?"

"Yes, please set it up."

Within one month of the initial diagnosis of this tumor in January 2007, Theo underwent life-threatening surgery to save his life.

Theo's youngest son came over from England for the surgery,

and he, Annette, and I sat in the waiting area for the doctor to come out with the good news.

"Theo is in recovery. We removed a thirty-pound tumor that was attached to each of the main organs in his abdomen. The tumor had to be cut away from each organ. His ureter was damaged in the process, and we had to put a stint in and repair his ureter; however, we see no problems with that in the long term. He will be in recovery for a couple of hours, and you can see him when he wakes up. He has fifty-six stitches down his chest and abdomen. I have a picture of the tumor. Would you like to see it?"

"Yes, I would." It was the largest mass of tissue I had ever seen. "Doctor, how could this have happened, given the yearly physicals?"

"This kind of cancer is an exceptionally soft mass of tissue, so unless you are having scans done, a physical exam will not discover it. The only reason this was discovered now is that there was a second harder cancerous tumor growing inside the soft tumor, and your doctor felt the harder tumor. He's lucky to be alive."

"Thank you, doctor. Will he need radiation or any other therapy to stop the cancer from returning?"

"No, radiation or chemotherapy do not work on this type of cancer. The only thing you can do is surgically remove it if it returns. You'll need to follow up every six months with scans to keep an eye on it."

It was a long recovery, but Theo finally returned to work as a professional truck driver about ten months after surgery. We had managed to maintain his personal truck during this time with God's help and provisions.

Then, almost two years after the first surgery, the doctor advised, "The cancer is back, and Theo, you'll need another surgery to remove the second batch of tumors."

The surgery happened, only this time, it was too much for Theo and his body. There were issues from the initial surgery and his ureter, and now, after the second surgery, there were other complications that made it impossible for Theo to return to work, and we sold his truck.

Theo was disabled; however, the social security administration did not think he was disabled, and Theo was too overwhelmed with everything to fight for disability benefits. We trusted that God would provide. God did provide, and Theo was my husband 'til death did he part.

CHAPTER FIVE–
THE NEW ME YEARS

HURRICANE ANDREW

It was late August of 1992, and it had been a calm summer for tropical activity. The first storm of the season was brewing in the Atlantic, and all eyes were on it. Everyone was praying that it would turn north and avoid Florida.

"Well, I wouldn't worry too much about that storm because they always turn north at the last minute," said Theo.

"This storm is not going to turn north. There's a high pressure to the north that will force it to turn west and continue straight across South Florida," I replied.

"Okay, then start putting up all the shutters now, gathering all of the storm preparations in an easy-to-access location, and follow the hurricane plans we have discussed numerous times. There is no way I can make it home in time to assist you. I am still in Northern California."

"Well, I also have to prepare my boss's house. Remember, he went on vacation with his wife and gave me the keys to his house."

"Then I would go over and secure his house now as best you can since no one is there, and then you can concentrate on our house until the storm arrives."

After that call, one of my brothers and I went to Mom's house to drop her awnings and make sure she was buttoned up for the storm. She did not want to stay at any of her son's homes or my home. She believed she would be safe where she was. We knew this storm was coming our way, and we needed as much time as possible to secure our homes.

On the way home, I went to my boss's house and did what I could to secure his home. Then I returned home.

My housemate went to secure his boss's home. Therefore, he was not available to help prepare our house and came home just in time for the initial bands of Hurricane Andrew.

I started all my preparations as I closely followed the news. Shutters went up, awnings went down, grills dragged into the house ready for use after the storm, tanks checked for gasoline, water containers filled, refrigerator and freezer turned to coldest temperatures, and boats filled with water to hold them down. These were some of the main preparations. We already had a small section in a closet for hurricane supplies like battery-powered radios, batteries, flashlights, important documents, candles, and other items needed if you have no power and cannot cook. The pantry was full of canned foods, snacks, and animal food.

Our neighbor across the street had no shutters for their house. I invited them to stay with us during the storm. There were seven of us hunkered down in the L-shaped hallway outside the two bedrooms and bathroom. The three dogs were locked in the bathroom, while the cats were locked in the bedroom. We prayed. We had a small battery-operated TV and watched Bryan Norcross advising us on what to expect and when to expect it.

The hurricane was moving fast, and the worst of the storm was over within eight hours. The worst was around 4:30 am. Starting around 1:00 am, we knew the awnings had been torn off the walls and the windows broken. The in-wall air conditioning units were gone. The storm tried to tear the doors open. This was the only protection for us in the hallway. The person nearest the door held onto it so it would not blow in. We could hear the shingle and tar ripping away from the roof, along with the sheetrock that comprised the ceiling. We had covered ourselves with twin mattresses. The carpet we were laying on was all wet.

We had parked two vehicles in the driveway with the windshields facing the direction of the storm winds. We parked the two other vehicles alongside those vehicles. All vehicles were filled with gasoline.

The power had gone out; however, we saw a bright light coming from the front yard; however, we did not know what it was. We were too scared to leave our position to go check it out. There was extreme thunder, lightning, and wind. It sounded like a freight train going over us and it was hurting our ears. The pressure on our ears was incredible.

Around 5:30 a.m., we felt like we had been through the worst and started to venture out from our cramped corner. We went to the front door and looked out the little window. One of the cars was on fire, and we were afraid it would explode with all the gasoline in those four cars. It was raining; however, the rain did not appear to be putting out the fire. We backed away from the door and returned to our protected area. Around 6:00 a.m., we went back to check on the fire. The car was no longer on fire.

We took the flashlights and started surveying the damage inside the home and checking out the holes in the roof. It was raining through the holes, the sheetrock was falling, and we carefully walked around those areas. We opened the bedroom doors and saw that the awnings, windows, and wall air-conditioning units were gone. We could not find our cats and let the dogs out of the bathroom. Everyone was scared.

Our neighbor decided they would venture out and check on their house. They had minimal damage even though they had no protection for their windows or doors. They were amazed. My house had extensive damage compared to theirs.

The car that was on fire during the storm had been struck by lightning. There was a large metal porch awning jammed underneath the front end of the car. The car was completely burned up to two inches from the gas tank. Everything past the gas tank was not burned. Had that car exploded, all the other cars around would have exploded and destroyed a sizable portion of the house. The vehicles were parked right up to the front of the house. We knew that God had spared us.

It is hard to explain the severity of the damage we saw in the neighborhood. Some houses had minor damage while others were damaged badly. The area we lived in took the northern part of the eyewall of Hurricane Andrew with confirmed winds above 160 mph, and we survived.

The first thing I wanted to do was to check on Mom. Mom lived about fifteen miles north of where I lived. As the power was out and the cell towers were destroyed, there was no cell phone service. I jumped into our dual-wheeled truck and made the drive to Mom's house. There was so much damage. Traffic lights hanging in the middle of the road, electrical wires everywhere, trees lying in the roads, buildings decimated, and gas stations buried made for a difficult drive. There were times when you could not even drive on the road and had to drive around trees or other debris. Massive trees were blocking the roads. I knew the truck would be able to negotiate the debris. There were no street signs, and it was extremely hard to navigate. All of your favorite landmarks no longer looked the same as before Hurricane Andrew. I made it to Mom's house and knocked on the door. The house looked like it had fared well. Mom answered the door, and we both were happy to see each other. I surveyed the house with her, and other than some landscape and tree debris, the house appeared fine. Mom did not have power like the rest of us; however, she had lots of flashlights and battery-operated lamps, and I knew she'd be okay. My next trip was to check on both of my brothers, who lived about five to ten miles south of where I lived.

Both of my brothers were okay. They had both experienced a portion of the eye of Hurricane Andrew as well as some of the eyewall, and their houses had more damage than mine. They were out checking on neighbors and helping others. After spending a little bit of time with them, I went back to my house.

When I got home, I started the arduous task of figuring out the most important things to do right then. My roommate and his girlfriend were already scheduled to move out the day after Hurricane Andrew, and they packed up his car and left. His car had lost a window and parts of a tree were sticking out of the car, but other than that damage, it was drivable. With them gone, I didn't have to worry about anyone but myself, and I started my recovery efforts.

I had no way of contacting Theo to let him know we were okay. A couple of days after the hurricane, one of the neighbors had gotten his hand on a satellite radio and I was able to call Theo and let him know that we were all okay. He was driving his way back to Florida from California, and it would be several more days before he arrived.

A week after Hurricane Andrew, I heard this loud noise that was not the sound of generators, and I looked up and saw Theo and his eighteen-wheeler truck. I started crying. Theo parked the truck in the middle of the road. I saw him looking at the house and watched as he dropped his head over the steering wheel and was crying. He got out of the truck, and we hugged. I told him it would be okay. We will rebuild. I had had a week to get used to the damage. I had not told him about the extent on the phone because I didn't want to upset him while he was driving.

That night, Theo told me that before arriving back in the State of Florida, his company had received a request from the State of Florida asking for volunteers to run supplies throughout the State for the Emergency Management Department. Theo told me the next day he would be heading south to a staging location to be loaded with supplies that he would deliver and then come back home. Apparently, he was the only truck driver in South Florida with a fifty-three-foot trailer, and it was in high demand.

The next day, Theo left to pick up his load. For over seven days, I did not hear from Theo and did not know what had happened to him. On battery-powered TVs, there were reports that trucks were being robbed of their supplies, and the Highway Patrol was now escorting these trucks with supplies. I was scared. When Theo finally came back home, I yelled at him. Theo told me there was nothing he could do because Emergency Management was given control of his supply loads, and he could not leave without their permission as Highway Patrol was keeping track of these trucks.

Hurricane Andrew happened on August 24, 1992. There was not a dry piece of furniture in the house. The mattresses were destroyed and placed on a trash pile at the front of the house, along with the wall-to-wall carpeting that had to be ripped up and removed the first day due to the noxious smell coming from the carpet mixing with the seawater and other contaminated water dumped by Hurricane Andrew. I put plastic garbage bags over the sofa and slept there every night. I remember having to go back to work with hose and heels two weeks after Hurricane Andrew. We had no electrical power for over six weeks. I needed a crowbar to get those nylon hose up my sweaty legs.

We did not receive any housing assistance until the day before Thanksgiving, almost three months after Hurricane Andrew. The insurance company finally provided a small RV trailer that we put beside the house to live in. We were so grateful we decided to have Mom over for Thanksgiving dinner.

Things were going well until the wind picked up and the canopy on the outside of the trailer was pulling on the trailer. We decided to close the canopy. As we were closing the spring-loaded canopy, my finger got caught on the railing, and it sliced it really badly. Mom used to be a nurse, so she put ice and pressure on it, and then we bandaged it and finished dinner.

The next day, I was still in a lot of pain, and when we went to change the bandage, we saw the finger did not look good. We went to the emergency room, and they said I had chopped through the bone and needed emergency surgery to save the finger. We went straight to the surgeon's office, where he cut off my wedding ring because there was no way to remove it as the finger was so swollen. Fifteen stitches later and a metal splint and my finger was better.

It took almost eighteen months to repair the home, and we lived in the trailer all that time. It was extremely tough dealing with the contractor, repairs, working full time, and Theo on the road because we could not afford for him to stay home. Again, God saw us through.

IN THE EYE OF THE STORM

"No, not again!"

My face contorted and twitched with each electrocution. Zap-zap, zappppp, zap-zap.

"Stop!"

It would not. I cried uncontrollably—that did not help. It only made the searing, stabbing, excruciating pain worse. No one was around to see me or help me.

It is called trigeminal neuralgia, a chronic pain condition that affects the trigeminal nerve from the brain to the eyes, the nose, and the mouth.

Symptoms include episodes of severe shooting or jabbing pain that may feel like an electric shock that can last from a few seconds to several minutes, lasting days, weeks, months, or longer, and become more frequent and intense over time.

A gust of wind, a sip of coffee, brushing my teeth, speaking, or a soft kiss can trigger a jolt of excruciating pain. With no cure available, neurologists are trying to manage it with seizure medicine.

Mark 4:35–41 (KJV) details when Jesus told the disciples to cross over to the other side. Obeying Jesus, the disciples set sail for the other side when "arose a great storm of wind, and the waves beat into the ship, so that it was now full. And he [Jesus] was in the hinder part of the ship, asleep on a pillow: and they awake him, and say unto him, Master, carest thou not that we perish? And Jesus arose, and rebuked the wind, and said unto the sea, Peace, be still. And the wind ceased, and there was a great calm. And he said unto them, Why are ye so fearful? How is it that ye have no faith?"

Trigeminal neuralgia is just one of the storms I live with daily.

I have had my neck reconstructed with a titanium plate, currently have three herniated discs in my lower back, have had my left knee operated on arthroscopically, and had my gallbladder removed on an emergency basis after it rotted and caused my gangrenous pancreas to poison my system, had a hysteroscopy on my uterus, been through stage 3 cancer requiring a radical double mastectomy, infusion chemotherapy, radiation therapy, oral chemotherapy, and hormone therapy. I will not lie, there are times when I have said, "God, don't You care that I'm in pain?"

I have prayed continually for God to heal me from all these ailments throughout my life, and I know that God has healed me from several of these ailments. Today, I am sixty-four years old as a result of God's healing and still living a strong, full life.

There have been times I believed I deserved some of this pain and suffering because of how I have lived my life. However, God's Word tells me that by Jesus Christ's stripes, He has already provided my healing. I just need to believe it, without a doubt, and walk in my healing. As long as I continue to doubt, even the slightest, or live in condemnation, I will not experience full healing.

Until I receive my full healing, either here on earth or in heaven, I know that Mark 4:35–41 confirms that God is with me always. Whether I am experiencing a metaphorical ship going down or searing, cattle-prodding zapping pain into my left cheek and mouth, or any other physical ailment I have experienced, are currently experiencing, or will experience in the future, I know that God is right there in the middle and the Holy Spirit is enduring all of this with me. He feels my pain, touches my tears, and cries with me.

．　．　．

The next "storm" that appeared in our lives was in 1995, while Theo was driving across America. I received a phone call.

"Is Theo Kohlasch there?"

"No, may I ask who's calling?"

"This is Sylvia with the U.S. State Department. Who am I speaking with?"

"This is Judy Kohlasch, Theo's wife. What can I help you with?"

"I'm calling to let Theo know that his mother passed away a week ago in England, and he needs to travel to England to claim her body and personal belongings."

"Well, Theo is driving across America right now. I can contact him by phone; however, I don't believe he has a valid passport, and I don't have any passport at all. What do we need to do?"

"Well, once you contact Theo, I will assist in getting valid passports for both of you. You will pick them up at the U.S. Embassy in England upon your arrival. You have twenty-four hours to pick them up."

"Thank you. May I call you back if we have any other issues?"

"Yes, here is my number."

I immediately called Theo to advise him that his "mother," which was really his grandmother, had passed away. Theo's mother was a U.S. citizen who had moved to England with Theo when he was fourteen years old.

"How fast can you get home? I need to make the travel arrangements."

"It will take me about two days to get home if I drive straight through. How are we going to pay for this?"

"I don't know, but I do know that God will provide."

I called my boss and advised him that I would be gone from the office for one week. He was not happy and insinuated that Theo could go alone and handle this without me. I told my boss that I was Theo's wife and he needed me.

Theo got home, and within eight hours of his arrival home, we were flying to England. The first thing we did was go to the U.S. Embassy to pick up our passports. Then we went to the hospital where his mother's body was being held. Theo went into the room and said goodbye to his mother, and asked them to perform the cremation as per her wishes.

We left the hospital and went to the apartment where she was staying. We knew that Theo's mom was experiencing health issues and was almost blind; however, we did not know the extent until we arrived at her apartment. We started sorting through all the paperwork, looking for important documents.

We talked about Theo's four children and discussed the fact that he should try and contact them and let them know about their grandmother and that he was in England for a couple of days. Theo had not seen his children for eleven years and he wasn't sure he had current phone numbers for them. International calling was extremely expensive.

Theo was able to contact his children, and we agreed to meet for dinner at a local pub. When the children arrived, it was extremely emotional. I was introduced to all of them with their current companions and children. Some of the children came over to assist with packing up their grandmother's belongings, finding places to donate items that could not be shipped to America, and planning for other items to be shipped back to America.

We arrived back in America a day late, as the last day in England was a British holiday, and we could not finalize our plans until the next day. My boss was extremely upset, even though I called him and advised him of the change in plans as soon as I found out about the British holiday.

It was hard for Theo to leave his children again; however, we told them that we would do whatever we could to assist them in traveling to America and spending time with us. Shortly thereafter, Theo's daughter and his middle son came to America to spend some time with us. They wanted to get visas to make travel from England to America easier in the future. We went to an immigration attorney who advised that the children would need to leave America and process visas from England. If they stayed in America, they could jeopardize their opportunity for visas in the future. We believed that since Theo was an American citizen, his children would be considered American citizens; however, we found out that was not true. America had an immigration law that stated that if the children of an American citizen were born in a foreign country five years after Theo's eighteenth birthday, they would be considered American citizens. However, since Theo's children were born prior to his twenty-third birthday, this meant they would have to go through the entire immigration process and obtain visas.

We spent several years in the immigration system getting visas for all four children. Some of the children were unable to get to the U.S. Embassy in London, England, to pick up their visas, and their visas expired.

Theo's youngest son (who is twenty-one years older than Annette) was able to get his visa, and he traveled to America and lived with us for several years. He subsequently got married, and he and his wife moved to England, where they had three children. Regrettably, Theo's son's visa expired. He and his wife thought it was best for his three children to move to America, as they have joint citizenship. His wife returned to America with the three children. Theo's son has just had his interview for his new visa to travel back to America as of the writing of this chapter. He has been away from his wife and children for over a year. Annette and I cannot wait for him to get back to America.

I have learned that God allows storms in our lives to show us that we can do anything if we rely on God and use His help. God's not testing us because He already knows we can do it with His help. Luke 18:27 (NIV) "Jesus replied, 'What is impossible with man is possible with God.'" We just need to remember this as we navigate every storm.

CAN'T AFFORD YOU

I had worked for Jacob, a sole practitioner, for ten years, excluding three months when I followed another attorney to another firm. I thought the grass would be greener at the new firm, only it was so burned and dead that I left and went back to the old firm. During my time with Jacob, he spent time mentoring me, believing in the abilities God had given me, and paying for my tuition to get my paralegal certificate. I went to night school for three years to get my paralegal certificate.

I used skills researching the law, writing draft pleadings, and drafting appellate briefs. I loved my job. It was hard, and I utilized all my skills. In addition to those skills, I also did billing and collections.

During those ten years, Jacob got divorced. It was a difficult divorce involving two children, and I tried to stay out of the fray. Then Jacob got remarried. Occasionally, I would work for his new wife on the weekends or at night. Then, his life with his second wife became seriously unstable. I stopped working for her after hours as I did not like what I was seeing. There were psychological issues that negatively impacted Jacob and, consequently, the firm.

One day, Jacob called me into his office. Jacob always called me into his office to discuss pending work, new clients, billing issues, and other items, so I did not suspect anything.

"You know I'm having marital issues."

"Yes," I replied.

"I cannot continue to keep the firm active anymore. I cannot afford you anymore, and I am closing down the firm. I am giving you two weeks to find another job. I will give you a great recommendation and respond to any prospective employer."

I was in shock. After ten years, how could he do this?

I went home that night, pulled out my resume, and immediately began looking through the legal help wanted ads. Two weeks to find another respectable job in this industry was unheard of.

I managed to find a job with some old attorneys I had previously worked with, along with Jacob, before he split off to form his own firm. I immediately applied. They already knew me, knew my work skills and work ethic, and I took the job. The worst thing about this new job was the commute. It was going to take me at least one to one and one-half hours each way to get to and from the job. It was like going from one end of the county to the other. You do what you must do, right?

I was grateful to have a paycheck and health insurance. The commute was difficult; however, Theo was always traveling. Since I was the only one living at home, I did not have to worry about leaving early in the morning or arriving home late. After about a year, the company transferred me from its northernmost office to a more reasonably situated office midway in the county. My commute would only take around forty-five minutes each way. I was incredibly happy.

Things at this firm started getting difficult, including not knowing if my paycheck would bounce or not, and I knew it was time to look for another job. As I was making the choice to find another job, I believed I wasn't under extreme pressure to simply take the next available job, or so I thought. It turned out my current job was getting dicey as the firm was imploding, and the senior partner was retiring and dismantling the firm.

The best thing that happened to me at this firm was I found a friend who needed a place to live, and I had a spare room in my house. Theo knew this friend, and he agreed that this would be a good thing to have a man around the house so I wasn't always alone. This friend moved in and lived with Theo and me for just over five years. Around the fourth year, his girlfriend moved in with us as well. The two of them were going to get married. They had found an apartment and were going to move out in late August 1992. Hurricane Andrew happened on August 24, 1992, and this was perfect because the house had been damaged so badly that there was no way all of us could continue to live in the house. The day after Hurricane Andrew, August 25, 1992, they moved out.

CHAPTER SIX–
THE SERVICE YEARS

WHAT'S FOR LUNCH?

It was lunchtime, and my husband and I were eating our prepared lunch on our screened-in porch. We had recently moved to Liberia, West Africa, as missionaries. Liberia, West Africa is a small country that was trying to re-establish itself after a long ten-year civil war. The amenities of life that Americans take for granted were a luxury in Liberia, including food, medical care, and social programs. There was electricity with a generator for four hours a day, contaminated running water that had to be boiled for everything you did, poverty, disease, and famine, and the closest "grocery store" was 125 miles away down the only winding "road" out of the mountains. Liberia did not have road maintenance or a department of transportation, and this "road" was like a farm road in America.

Across the road next to our house in the compound were two young boys who caught my attention.

"He's up that tree," yelled Sumo, a thirteen-year-old Liberian boy, pointing to a bushy tree beside the narrow, dirt road.

"I'm going up," said George, his twelve-year-old brother.

"Do you see him, Sumo?"

"Yeah, he is on that branch. To the left of you," pointed Sumo.

"Light the fire. He will have to jump, and you can get him."

"Okay," said Sumo, as he lit the match, threw it in the base, and blew to make the flames grow.

"Is it burning?"

"Yeah, it's smoking good."

"Okay, I am going after him. If he falls or jumps, you get him."

"Okay, George. Do not worry, we'll get him," said Sumo as George climbed after the little brown squirrel. Their teamwork revealed they had done this before.

I finally saw the young squirrel they were chasing, and my thoughts immediately said, "Wait, what are they doing to that poor squirrel? Should I go out there and stop them?"

"George, he jumped to the other branch," said Sumo through thick gray smoke.

"I saw him. I'll cross over," said George as he jumped across the two-foot distance between the branches.

"Sumo, get ready. He is ready to jump."

"I'm ready."

"Sumo, he is down. Do you see him?"

"Get him, Sumo."

"I'm trying."

"Hurry, Sumo. I am coming."

"I got him. I got him," yelled Sumo, holding the squirrel up by the tail as George

jumped to the ground.

"Where's our stick?"

"Oh my gosh, what are they going to do to that squirrel?" I said to Theo.

"Do not interfere. We are guests here," replied Theo.

"I got it," yelled George as he picked up a one-inch-thick stick.

"Put him on the ground. I will do him."

"Okay," said Sumo as George hit the squirrel with the stick.

"He's dead," said Sumo.

I could not believe what I had just seen. How could they torture that little squirrel?

"Mom's gonna be happy we got meat for the stew. Let's get home," said Sumo, who ran off with George behind.

My concern for the squirrel was so misplaced. I did not see

the hungry boys who wanted to surprise their mother with meat for the stew. All the while this was going on, we were enjoying the lunch that someone had prepared for us.

George and Sumo lived in Liberia, West Africa. In 2000, when my husband and I were there, Liberia was a country slightly larger than the state of Tennessee, with approximately 3.3 million people. Over 80 percent of the people lived below the poverty level, with little or no money and few or no things they owned. In 2002, the United Nations published a report finding only one country in the world with worse poverty than Liberia.

Can you imagine living in one of the poorest countries in the world? When you ask, "Hey, Mom, what's for lunch?" do you think your mother would say, "How about McDonald's or Burger King?" What if your mother asked you to get lunch? Where would you go? What would you bring home?

In Liberia, there's no McDonald's or Burger King. No fast food. Want to eat? You can grow food or buy food, but you need money to do both since you need seeds and grain to grow food. If you do not have money to grow food, how do you eat? What do you eat?

For George and Sumo, squirrel soup was on the menu that day. What is on the menu every day? That was an everyday question because there was limited electricity for the missionaries and some Liberians who lived on the compound, but Liberians did not have refrigerators.

Liberians ate cooked rice for breakfast, lunch, and dinner. Rice filled up an empty stomach, but without meat, chicken, fish, or other protein, it did not provide your body with what it needed to stay healthy and strong. Every day, young Liberian children hunted for meat, chicken, fish, or any other protein-packed food, such as deer, snake, chicken feet, fish, monkey, and squirrel.

Liberia did not have grocery stores like America; therefore, outdoor markets were where they bought food. If Sumo and

George had killed two squirrels that day, they probably would have sold one squirrel in the market and eaten one.

Did you not catch a squirrel today? Well, chicken feet made good Liberian soup. That is right, chicken feet. Liberians sold chickens to businessmen or foreign merchants who didn't want the feet. Liberians would buy back the feet for soup.

Are you thinking, wow, I wish I could go hunting for food all day long rather than going to school? Well, many Liberian children do not even have that choice. Most Liberians cannot afford school because the tuition costs and required uniforms are too expensive. There, education is secondary to finding food for survival. Therefore, only 57.5 percent of Liberians over the age of fifteen can read and write. Uneducated Liberians comprised 74 percent of the population who worked in the country's agriculture industry growing rubber trees, coffee, cocoa, rice, cassava (which is tapioca), palm oil, sugarcane, bananas, sheep, goats, and timber.

In contrast, 97 percent of American people over age fifteen can read and write, and only 2 percent work in agriculture. In America, we would rather buy our food than grow it.

In Liberia, growing food was also particularly important. Consequently, the average Liberian woman had six children who helped harvest fields. Why so many children? The average Liberian lived only forty-eight years. The average American lived seventy-eight years. Why the stark difference? Lack of clean water and healthy food are the main reasons. Sadly, three of every six children would die before the age of fifteen due to malnutrition, hunger, or illness. I could not even imagine that half of one's family would be dead shortly after turning teenagers.

Liberia completely changed my view on life and how to appreciate the blessings from God and living in America. Luke 12:29–31 (NLT) says, "And don't be concerned about what to eat and what to drink. Don't worry about such things. These things dominate the thoughts of unbelievers all over the world, but your Father already knows your needs. Seek the Kingdom of God above all else, and he will give you everything you need."

What I originally saw and thought was two young boys being mean to an innocent squirrel. The truth was I saw God provide sustenance for a family and two young boys doing their part to help feed their family. God showed me why I should not judge people when I don't know the truth. Only God knows the truth.

ME PLUS ONE

After Theo and I had been married for sixteen years, Theo applied for a missionary position in Liberia, West Africa. Theo had four children from a prior marriage, and they all lived in England. Theo was already a grandfather, which made me a grandmother through marriage.

Theo received the assignment, and we were off to Liberia, West Africa, to help rebuild an African hospital that had been destroyed during the ongoing civil war. Hospitals in Africa are like small-town AIDS clinics in America: exceedingly small, ill-equipped, and full of sick, malnourished, dying people.

Well, I know the Bible says God's timing is perfect, and I try to believe that, but sometimes I question it. This was one of those times.

Anticipating we would be missionaries for an extended period of time, we sold our house, gave our car away to Mom, Theo sold his business tractor-trailer, and we gave away most of our belongings, believing it would be worthless when we came back to America and definitely not worth storing.

We arrived in Liberia and were assigned to a compound house up in the mountains. Hiring Liberians to assist us with our compound housing provided much-needed funds for Liberians to provide for their families. We had a cook, a cleaner, a security guard, and a handyman for the house.

Edward was on duty at our house that quiet, dark, starry night. We really didn't need a security guard; however, it was a way to help Edward earn money for his family, wife, and his seven-year-old son. I awoke at dawn and watched a glorious sunrise. I took my cup of coffee to our porch to join Edward.

"Did anything happen last night?" I queried.

"Nothing out of the ordinary," reported Edward.

Then, out of nowhere, Edward asked, "Why don't you have any children?"

Startled by the abrupt question, I quickly retorted in defense, "Well, technically, I do have children, four stepchildren. Three boys and a girl."

"Aren't those Theo's children?

"Yes."

"Where are your children?"

"I do not know. We've been married for sixteen years, and God has not provided me with any children. I do not know if I can even have children."

"I will get the tribal priests and spiritual healers to pray that God will open your womb. I have a book that might help. I will bring it tonight when I come on duty."

"Okay, Edward. I'll look forward to reading it."

For the rest of the day, I reported to the hospital administration, focusing on assisting the hospital administrator with budgets, letters, emails, and reports to the various government NGOs (non-governmental organizations). The day went by quickly, and I returned home for dinner and rest. I really did not think Edward would show up with a book, as they are extremely rare in Liberia. Bibles are everywhere because lots of NGOs donate Bibles, but reading literature was almost impossible to find, much less for a Liberian to afford.

Edward reported for work at 6:00 p.m. sharp.

"Here's the book I was telling you about this morning," handing the paperback book to me with a big smile.

I read the title, "'Spiritual Pregnancy'?"

"Yes. You read it and let me know what you think."

I started reading that book because we had lights thanks to the generator; however, I knew the lights would go out in a couple of hours. We had four hours of electricity a night. We savored every minute. I got up early the next morning to read in the sunlight before work. I was really intrigued and captivated by the words.

"You have not because you do not ask. Ask, and you shall receive, seek and you shall find, knock and the door shall be opened, but you have to ask without wavering, believing in your heart that God will provide what you ask for."

I continued reading the book that night because the words I read were accurately describing the longings of my heart, even though I had never told anyone how much I yearned for a child.

I remember when I got married, Theo said, "I don't want any more children, and if you get pregnant, I'll divorce you."

Those words reverberated in my mind for sixteen years.

I finished the book that night using flashlights because I could not put it down until I reached the end. Finally, someone understood how I felt and was able to put it into words and provide godly advice and prayers.

I started secretly praying for a child every day for about a month without telling Theo or Edward about my communications with my heavenly Father, Jehovah Jireh, my Provider. It was time for my menstruation, and I was spotting and feeling sick with fever, chills, pain, and nausea. I went to the hospital, and it was confirmed—I had malaria! Again! Every day, I took my anti-malaria pills, and now I was having my second bout of malaria. Theo never took his anti-malaria pills. He gave them to his Liberian friends.

I was prescribed antibiotics and ordered to go back to bed. For two days, I lay in bed, but I was not getting better. The nausea was horrible; the spotting was replaced with dark red blood. It did not seem normal. The abdominal pain kept me in a fetal position most of the time.

The next day, after waiting three months, the compound had just received its massive container shipment of supplies, and all hands were on deck to unload the medical supplies and other necessary items shipped from the United States.

I got dressed and went to find Dr. Gina, one of the other missionaries from America. Excitedly, she was taking inventory of all the items that had arrived in the container.

"Dr. Gina, you know I've been sick with malaria. I do not feel right, and my nausea has increased to the point I'm throwing up during and after dinner. I have extreme abdominal pain, and I'm bleeding, and it's not normal for me. I know this is a strange request; however, would you have a pregnancy test?"

"You are in luck. We just received pregnancy tests in the shipment. I just saw them over here. Here you go."

"Thank you. I'll let you know what it says."

I immediately returned home and took the test.

There was a plus sign on the white stick with the little window in the middle.

"Does this mean I'm pregnant?" I asked myself. I went to Dr. Gina to confirm by showing her the stick.

"Congratulations, you're pregnant."

"Thanks, I think. Now what?

"Well, with that bleeding, I think we should do an ultrasound to confirm you're pregnant, the age of the fetus, and see if there are any medical issues we should be aware of. I will schedule the ultrasound for this afternoon."

"Thank you," I said. Pensively walking away, my thoughts immediately began fearfully attacking me. *Oh, no, it cannot be. What will Theo say when I tell him? Will he divorce me?*

I walked around the compound searching for Theo and ran into Sumo, the compound's resident electrician.

"Do you know where Theo is?"

"He's at the maintenance building."

"Thanks."

I was not in any hurry to get to the maintenance building. *What will I say? How will I tell Theo? How can I have a child at my age? Forty-one-year-old women do not have children except God-blessed, righteous Sarah, Abraham's wife!* I was not Sarah!

I arrived at the maintenance building, waving at Theo to come over.

"What's up? Why are you here? You're supposed to be in bed."

"Well, you know I've been really sick with malaria, and my nausea and bleeding got worse, so I went and saw Dr. Gina."

"So, what did she say?"

"Theo, what would you say if I told you I was pregnant?" I blurted out.

"Well, I guess I'd say we're having a child."

"Theo, I'm pregnant."

"What? How do you know? Are you sure?"

"Yes, when I went to see Dr. Gina, I got a pregnancy test from her, and it was positive." I pulled the test out of my pocket.

"Dr. Gina wants to do an ultrasound this afternoon because of my bleeding and other symptoms. They want to determine how old the fetus is and see if there are any issues, as I should not be bleeding and pregnant at the same time. Will you go to the ultrasound with me this afternoon?"

"Yes, I'll go." Theo's hesitancy was palpable. I found a stool at the maintenance building, deciding to wait for the ultrasound there, as it was closer to the hospital than our house.

An hour later, Dr. Gina found me at the maintenance building, "It's time for the ultrasound."

We arrived at the hospital, which was no larger than a clinic in the United States, and I was escorted to an operating room.

"Lay down and get comfortable. This should not hurt." The ultrasound technician positioned her stool next to my right side as I lay flat on the table, and Dr. Brown, the resident general physician, stood by.

The wand moved across my belly. "Boom, boom, boom, boom, boom. There it is. That is the heartbeat."

I saw red flitters on the screen, watching the fetus' heart pump blood. "Is that inside me? Is that a child?"

"Yes, that is your child. That fetus is ten weeks old. Everything looks okay. Congratulations to both of you. It is a girl." Dr. Brown confirmed the observations on the screen.

"Look at that little Beepsicle," said Theo. "She's so little."

We left that ultrasound speechless and in shock.

That shock was still fresh in our minds when Dr. Gina came over to the house to talk to Theo and me.

"I have spoken with Dr. Brown, Mr. Smith (the missionary hospital administrator I worked with), our missionary leader in America, and the Pastor of your home church in America. Given the second bout of malaria Judy has right now, the bleeding she is experiencing, and her advanced maternal age, we believe Judy needs to leave Liberia immediately. She needs to be seen by specialists in America to treat her malaria and protect her fetus. We have arranged for Judy to fly out tomorrow. Please do not tell any Liberians about the pregnancy, and if anyone asks, just tell them she went home due to medical complications. Do you have any questions for me?"

Fighting through the tears, I was having a tough time focusing on the present situation, stumbling through the endless fog of fear. "What about Liberia? What about Theo? How can I do this? I have no place to live, no car, no job, nothing. My mom will never let me live with her, given how angry she was when I left for Liberia." The joy of the most precious gift in the world was being crushed by endless insecurity and fear.

"How can you abandon your seventy-nine-year-old mother to go work with people in another country you don't even know? Go, and do not ever come back," were her last words to me.

"Do not worry about those things. Christina, one of your fellow church members, has offered a room in her home for you to live in. She has a spare vehicle you can drive. Judy, you should try and contact your prior employer and see if you can get your job back. You've only been gone six months, and they might take you back. You can email them using the hospital administrator's computer. Get packed today. Since it will take an hour and one-half to get to Monrovia, the driver will take you to Monrovia at 8:00 a.m. tomorrow morning. Your flight leaves at 12:30 p.m. See you tomorrow morning to say goodbye."

I never had a chance to say goodbye to any Liberians. I do not know if they ever found out the truth about why I left so quickly. My prior employer did take me back, knowing I was pregnant, and I lived with Christina, preparing to become a single mom. Theo remained in Liberia.

I made the long trip home, scared and alone but blossoming on the inside with the knowledge that I had a young life growing inside me. I was still in shock, scared of the future, and wondering what kind of a mother I would be.

God paved the way to Liberia, West Africa, and I knew He would pave the way back to America. I arrived back in America and was able to return to my old job as a Legal Secretary with the same firm. They had trouble finding a replacement for me while I was gone.

I rented a room with Christina because Mom wanted nothing to do with me or my baby. Christina had a two-year-old daughter, and I was grateful she opened her home for us. I immediately got prenatal care and treatment for my malaria and did the best I could to prepare life for my daughter.

Before I left Liberia, Theo and I had to pick out a name for our child. I wanted and prayed for a child, and God heard my prayers. Matthew 7:7 (KJV) says, "**A**sk, and it shall be given you; [**S**]eek, and ye shall find; [**K**]nock, and it shall be opened unto you." I knew I wanted her initials to spell **ASK** so that she and I would always remember how she came into this world. My middle name was Ann, and I had a distinguished role model back in America named Annette. We decided her first name would be Annette. As God blessed me with a child at such an old age as Abraham's wife, Sarah, Theo and I agreed her middle name would be Sarah. Our child was named "Annette Sarah Kohlasch."

With infectious disease specialists, OB-GYN specialists, and other medical specialists guiding me through my pregnancy, Annette Sarah arrived a month early, perfectly healthy and normal, other than an innocent heart murmur, exactly one day shy of a year after leaving for Liberia, West Africa. What a year that had been. Those six months of living in Liberia, West Africa, were the most interesting and life-changing of my entire life, and I will never forget them.

CAN'T AFFORD YOU, AGAIN!

After being let go by the sole practitioner, Jacob, I found a job looking for a Legal Secretary rather than a Paralegal, and I applied. I went for the interview and Mr. D had done his homework on me. He had checked on all the prior companies I worked for, including checking on my bachelor's degree and my Paralegal Certificate.

"Can you do dictation?" Yes, back then shorthand and dictation were still a thing. We did not have all the technology of today, and Mr. D was not technologically minded.

"Yes."

"Can you work long hours?"

"Yes."

"Good because I usually work six to seven days a week, and I need someone to be here during that time."

"Well, I do not work on Sundays because that's the Lord's Day; however, I can give you time the other days of the week."

"I see you have a paralegal certification; however, I do not need a paralegal as we already have two paralegals in the firm. Would you be willing to work as a legal secretary?"

"Yes." It appeared at this firm, the legal secretary was paid more than the paralegal anyway.

"You know one of your prior bosses did not give you a great recommendation. He said you had some issues dealing with clients, so if I agree to hire you, it will be on a probationary basis, and it will not be for more money than you are currently making. If you work out, every year in December we have annual reviews, and we can reevaluate everything then if you are still here."

I finished the interview and hoped that I would get this job since there was not much time to find another job. I was hired in March. I was working six days a week, working around sixty hours per week. There were five other attorneys in the firm and two paralegals to begin with. Everything I did for Mr. D was through dictation; it was hard and challenging, but I liked it. Thank goodness I was hourly because without a pay raise from the prior job, making ends meet was difficult. December came around, and everyone got their reviews and their pay raises, except me. I went to my boss.

"Mr. D, I see that reviews occurred, and I did not get a pay raise. You told me that if I made it through my probationary period to December, you would review me and increase my pay if appropriate. You stated that I have been doing a fantastic job for you; however, I didn't get a pay raise. Why not?"

"Reviews do happen yearly; however, you are not eligible for a pay raise unless you have been here a full year and received a good review. You have only been here ten months. Your next review for salary increase will not occur until next December."

"You mean I must wait twenty-two months before I can be reviewed for a salary increase? You did not tell me that when I interviewed with you."

"But I did. I told you we do annual reviews, and you have not been here for a year."

I walked out of his office and went back to my desk in shock. What could I do? Looking for another job in this tight industry was not on the table for me. I put my head down and did what God wanted me to do. The next December, I was reviewed and got a $.50 per hour pay raise after twenty-two months.

In May of 2000, my husband and I received a calling to go to Liberia, West Africa, as missionaries. I informed my boss that in June 2000, I was leaving. He wished me good luck.

In February of 2001, I became pregnant and had to leave Liberia, West Africa, because I had malaria, was bleeding, and was of advanced maternal age (AMA), as the medical profession calls it. The Evangelical Church that sent us to Africa was afraid that I could lose the baby. Where we were working, there were no obstetricians, no specialized doctors, only general physicians. I came home to America.

While I was gone, Mr. D could not keep an assistant and had gone through six. I had stayed connected with one of the attorneys while in Africa, and she told me to ask for my job back. I contacted Mr. D, told him I was coming home pregnant, and asked if he needed a secretary. He told me I could start work as soon as I arrived back in America.

In August of 2001, I had Annette at the age of forty-two, was out on maternity leave for twelve weeks, and returned to work. Mr. D. was kind and understanding. When I had to work overtime and could not get to the daycare to pick up Annette on time, he would pay the $1.00 per minute late fee. When I had to work on Saturdays, holidays, or days when Annette was not in daycare, he allowed me to bring her to work. My cubicle area was so large he brought a little TV and a mat for her to make a little camp underneath my desk where she could play, sleep, or watch TV while I worked. Annette loved it. She had so much fun. Mr. D and his wife did not have any children, and he loved Annette. Annette grew up at that firm.

Then, in late December of 2010, I had an MRI of my neck because I was having pain and numbness in my right arm. The day after the MRI was taken, I received a call.

"Ms. Kohlasch, you need to schedule an appointment with your doctor immediately. Please call them. They will see you on an emergency basis."

"What's going on?"

"We cannot tell you. You just need to get in to see your doctor."

"Okay, I will."

I hung up the phone and called Theo. The appointment was scheduled for the next day, December 29, 2010, the day before Theo's birthday. I was already scheduled to take the day off to celebrate Theo's birthday. Theo, Annette, and I arrived at the doctor's office and were taken into a room.

"Good morning, everyone. We have the results back from your MRI you took yesterday." The doctor put the MRI films up on the lighted screens.

"This is your spinal cord. It is being strangled to the point that it is cutting off circulation to your left arm. You need emergency surgery. If you have the slightest bump, fall, or accident, you could become a quadriplegic. We'd like to schedule the surgery today." The doctor continued discussing the procedure, what needed to be done, how it was going to happen, and the recovery time, as well as the potential risks of quadriplegia.

I was in shock, and I knew I needed to compose myself and think rationally.

"I need time to process this. You see, I have a nine-year-old daughter, and my husband and I need to put things in order before I have any surgery."

We went home. The next day, December 30, 2010, we arrived at the Emergency Room. I was immediately taken to a room, and the surgery was scheduled for the next day, December 31, 2010. The surgery was extremely successful, replacing two cadaver vertebrae for my damaged vertebrae. A titanium plate with six screws held the new vertebrae in place and stabilized my neck, removing the impingement on the spinal cord.

Two weeks later, I went back to work, not requiring any physical therapy or follow-up procedures. I was excited to be back at work. My phone rings.

"Judy, can you come into my office?"

I hung up the phone and went into my boss's office. I sat down in front of his desk.

"You know you are my highest-paid employee, and business has been declining. I am going to have to let you go. I will work with you by responding to future employment inquiries, but I ask that you secure other employment quickly."

Excluding the six months in Africa as a missionary, I worked for Mr. D for fourteen years. I had been there through lots of personnel changes, the death of the senior partner, and other upheaval similar in companies. All the paralegals who were there when I first arrived were gone, and I had been doing both paralegal and legal secretary work at the pay rate of a legal secretary. When I started at the firm, there was a young girl who was the receptionist. She subsequently was promoted and became a legal secretary with me. We were the only two assistants for the five attorneys. I trained her for the position and trained her on how to do paralegal work. She asked her boss to certify her as a registered paralegal, and her boss did. Fourteen years later, she was now a registered paralegal. I tried to get certified as a registered paralegal; however, my boss would not sign the paperwork after fourteen years.

It was happening again. I walked out of Mr. D's office in total shock. The total amount of all the raises amounted to approximately $210 per year, which was equivalent to $4.00 a week. Remember, I was usually working six days a week, making time and a half. My salary could not have been the reason. Then I helped Mr. D fight (through correspondence and phone calls) over two lamps he bought from France totaling $60,000, which was well over my salary, and here he was saying he couldn't afford me. I was angry and hurt. How could he? Loyalty meant nothing!

It was back to the job hunt, looking for anything and everything. Then, when I had a prospective employer call for a recommendation, Mr. D was not nice, according to my new employer.

CHAPTER SEVEN –
THE WILDERNESS YEARS

STEVE'S RISE AND FALL

"Hey Steve, I thought you would like to meet your two-month-old niece. May I come over?"

"Sure, come on over."

I got dressed, changed my daughter's diaper, strapped her in the car, and headed over to Steve's place.

Steve met me at the door, gave me a big hug, and we went in. Steve always said he did not have much to give since he became disabled; however, hugs were free, and he gave some great bear hugs. It had been a while since I had seen Steve, and with my impending divorce, I needed a bear hug.

"How are you doing? What have you been doing?"

"Been in a lot of pain, and my doctor has reduced my pain medicine. I am not sure how I'll survive, but I'm still here today."

"What will you do if he cuts you off? Are there alternative medicines that would work?"

"I do not know, but I won't be here when that happens. I've told you and other family members for years that if that happens, I will kill myself. There is not a lot in my life worth living for."

"Well, you are a new uncle, and I would like my daughter to know her Uncle Steve. Do you want to hold her?"

I placed her on his lap while he sat in his recliner and he played with her fingers and bounced her, and she was enjoying it.

We finished catching up and I told him about my upcoming divorce, and then I left.

About ten days later, my phone rang.

"Hey, Joe. What is up?"

"I have some bad news to tell you about Steve."

"Is he dead?" I asked.

"Yes," said Joe.

Steve was highly intelligent and lived a hard life. He was kicked out of the house around seventeen or eighteen years old. He does not remember why, but one day, he came out of the bathroom, and Mom told him, "Get out of my house. Now."

My mom had ordered all of us remaining siblings to take all of Steve's belongings and throw them in the front yard. I had learned to "obey my mother" or get another beating. I complied. When Steve walked onto the front porch, he was shocked. I was crying as I watched Steve pick up his stuff quickly, throw it in the trunk and back seat of his car, get in his car, and drive off. I wondered if I would ever see Steve again.

Steve dropped out of high school because he was bored with the lessons. He did not believe he was learning anything. Then, he gets kicked out of the house. While he never returned to high school, I do not know a lot about what happened to him after that, but I heard he lived in his car for a while, got his GED, got a job working for the County, and moved into an apartment with roommates.

The next time I remembered seeing my brother, he had a girlfriend for a couple of years, had a best friend from work who was married, and life was going well for him, at least that's what I thought. He suffered from incurable health issues because of his girlfriend not being faithful to him. He spent a lot of time at his best friend's house because his wife would cook dinner for them.

Then, his best friend was seriously injured when a draw bridge he was repairing was inadvertently closed with him under the bridge. The bridge crushed him between the heavy metal slabs before anyone realized he was there, totally disabling him for life.

I am not sure of the exact details; however, about three to four years later, my other brother, Joe, met the same fate as Steve when Mom kicked him out of the house with all his belongings. He too lived in his car for a while.

Joe and I were remarkably close. Joe was one year older than me; however, we had been in the same grade for years as Mom had kept Joe back one year during elementary school. Joe was tall and strong, and he would always protect me. Joe and I had endured the wrath of Mom for years together.

Joe also got a job with the County and, at some point, got an apartment with Steve and another roommate from high school. Both Steve and Joe witnessed not one but two suicides during the time they lived together. I cannot imagine the emotional turmoil that created in their lives.

ASSISTED LIVING

Mom, living all alone in her house, would call me at all hours of the day and night. She was experiencing some dementia and was still grieving over Steve's suicide. Steve was her favorite child. They say parents should not have favorites; however, that does not always happen. Steve was the closest in personality to Mom than any of us other siblings.

One night, she told me, "People are coming into my house and removing things. I found my walker on top of the car."

Mom would get scared and call 911. They reported her to Elder Services, who did a field check and reported that she was no longer able to reside alone.

Neither my brother nor I knew about any of these calls to 911 or the visit of Elder Services.

I would go over to Mom's house to check on her, pay her bills, and make sure she was doing okay. I would take her grocery shopping or go to the bookstore or the library because she loved to read books.

One day, I saw her mail and it was a letter from Elder Services. Mom was ordered to get in-home care or move to a nursing facility.

As my brother and I were the only family members close by, we helped Mom get some in-home care; however, Mom was not happy with them. We thought things were okay.

Elder Services did another site visit and found Mom was not being cared for with in-home care.

"Mom, where is your in-home care?"

"The nurses were stealing from me. They were not taking care of me, so I fired them."

Elder Services ordered that Mom be moved to a nursing facility within thirty days.

My brother and I found an assisted living facility (ALF) where she would have her own room and eat her meals together with other residents, and it had twenty-four-hour nursing care. We were going to have to sell her home to pay the expenses, as Medicare would not cover these expenses.

My brother and I started sorting through the four-bedroom, two-bath house that my mother had lived in for approximately forty-seven years. We were doing this at night because I was still working full-time, divorced, and Annette was a toddler by now. We put the house up for sale and wondered how we would get it sold in time and pay off the reverse mortgage.

God stepped in, and the next-door neighbor said that they would buy the house and pay cash. We knew we were selling it below market value, but getting funds to take care of Mom was more important. Within thirty days, the house was sold, and Mom was living in the ALF with the modern furniture we helped her buy, along with a motorized scooter to assist her in getting around, as she had become physically unstable.

Annette and I would go almost every weekend to see Mom at the ALF, who was miserable. Grandma would put Annette on her lap and drive her around the ALF. We'd have lunch with Mom, and she would always give Annette soup and crackers.

"You have such a strong, loving relationship with Annette. It's beautiful to see. The two of you are a joy to watch. You know I could never show affection or praise to any one of you because then the others would become jealous. It was hard."

I finally got the answer to why Mom never hugged me or gave me any other feelings of love.

Mom would tell me, "I do not like it here. I do not like the staff. I want to leave."

"Mom, you cannot leave here. You created this situation with all the calls to 911, firing the home health staff, and refusing to comply with certain restrictions. I wish we could do something different; however, I do not see that happening given the circumstances."

Mom did not want to hear any of that. About a year after living there, the ALF called me.

"Your mom has fallen and broken her hip and is in the hospital having surgery to get a titanium hip. She will have to be placed in a rehabilitation hospital after surgery because we are only a minimally assisted living facility and cannot provide the assistance she needs after surgery."

While she was at the rehabilitation hospital, Annette, my brother, and I would visit her at different times. As angry and miserable as she was at the ALF, she was just as angry and miserable at the rehabilitation hospital; however, she survived and returned to the ALF.

Almost one year to the day, my mother fell again at the ALF and broke the other hip. We went through the same situation with the rehabilitation hospital. She finally returned to the ALF.

On Thanksgiving Day 2006, I received a call from the ALF.

"Your mother has been taken to the hospital with abnormal bleeding."

I immediately left work and went to the hospital.

For the second time in her life, she received a second diagnosis with two tumors in her bladder. She had previously been diagnosed with bladder cancer. She had undergone surgery and they cut out the tumor, and she had been cancer-free until now.

"I refuse to have my bladder removed at this age. Just let me die."

Mom returned to the ALF under hospice care.

I contacted all the living family members and advised them of the current situation. They agreed to all meet at the ALF. Most of the family members had not seen Mom in years, and this would be their last visit.

December 2006 was when Theo and I got remarried, and then Theo received his cancer diagnosis. I talked to Mom about all of this to get her mind off her pain. Watching someone die is heartbreaking and painful.

Mom was happy that Theo and I had remarried.

"I have a good feeling about Theo's surgery, and he's going to be okay," she told me during one of my visits.

Mom died on February 27, 2007, almost thirty days after Theo's surgery. It was like she was waiting for Theo to survive so she could die.

It was 5:30 a.m. on the morning of February 27, 2007, when the phone rang.

"Your mom passed away this morning. We need to move the body to the coroner's office. Will you be coming down?"

"Yes, I will be down as soon as possible. Please do not remove the body, as I want to say goodbye."

I immediately called my brother. He was closer to the ALF than I was, and he knew I had Theo at home recovering from surgery.

"I'll go down and deal with the ALF."

When my brother arrived at the ALF, they ignored my wishes and had already released the body to the coroner's office.

Shortly after Mom's death, my brother and I went down to the ALF and gave away some of Mom's belongings to staff members who were especially nice to her and then removed the rest of her belongings. It was hard to explain to Annette that we would no longer visit Grandma, and she would no longer ride on the scooter and share soup and crackers with Grandma.

Annette was also dealing with Dad recovering from surgery. This was such a double-whammy for Annette.

WHERE ARE YOU HEADING?

"Hurry up, Annette,"

"I'm coming, Mom!" Annette panted as she ran through the half-empty asphalt parking lot. Her favorite royal-blue princess dress waved behind her like wings on a butterfly. "Do you know where to go, Mom?"

"No, but I have the address, so I have an idea where I'm going."

"Mom, we cannot be late! We will miss seeing friends and the presents and cake."

Tears ran down Annette's heat-flushed face. "How will you find the house?" she asked, wiping her eyes and pushing hair away from her face.

"Don't worry, Annette. The address tells me where Kylee lives."

"Mom, call Kylee's mom for directions!"

"I do not need to, Annette. I can find the house!" I turned the car right and headed out.

Annette rolled her window up and down and fidgeted in her seat. The ride seemed endless.

"We're here."

I parked in the sun-scorched grass in front of the pale pink house with white trim.

"Roll up your window."

"Hurry, Mom!" Annette got out of the car and slammed her door.

"Let's go."

How did I know where I was going? I knew where I was, what direction I was facing, and what direction I needed to go based on a compass or GPS. But what if I did not have a compass or GPS? Could I still figure out where to go?

SEEING THE HAND OF GOD

Native Indians and early settlers used the sun for direction during the day. How? They knew the sun rose in the east and set in the west. By looking at the sun, they could tell which way they were traveling. If the sun were on their right in the morning, they were traveling north. If it was on their right in the afternoon, they were traveling south.

Like the sun, a compass, or a GPS, the Bible, God's Word, tells us which way we're going and which way we should be heading. The Bible contains God's always-truthful, never-changing rules and guidelines for our lives. By reading, learning, and using the Bible, we can determine where we are in God's world and where He wants us to be.

Have you ever asked yourself,

"Am I headed in the wrong direction? Do I know what is true or what's false? Am I in conflict with God or His Word?"

Not sure? The Bible can answer these questions and more.

In Psalm 32:8 (NLT), "The LORD says, 'I will guide you along the best pathway for your life. I will advise you and watch over you.'" All of us must go through challenging times, and God is always there to help.

You catch yourself asking, "Okay, but which way should I go?"

Check out God's promise to his people in Isaiah 30:19–21 (NLT), "...He will be gracious if you ask for help. He will surely respond to the sound of your cries. Though the Lord gave you adversity for food and suffering for drink, he will still be with you to teach you. You will see your teacher with your own eyes. Your own ears will hear him. Right behind you, a voice will say, 'This is the way you should go' whether to the right or to the left."

Who is your teacher? Who are you following? Are you following the truth or lies? Let God show you right and wrong. Psalm 119:11 (NLT) says, "I have hidden Your word in my heart, that I might not sin against you."

Do you know where you are heading?

. . .

After returning to America from Liberia, I did not know where my life was heading, but I was trusting God. I communicated with Theo mostly by email and was experiencing extraordinary joy about Annette but uneasiness and sadness about my marriage. The tone of the emails was distant, lacking any excitement, and somewhat negative. The only thing I could think to do was pray.

The church missionary leader in America arranged for Theo to return home two weeks after Annette was born despite his petitions to remain in Liberia. Theo had found his niche in life and had fallen in love with Liberia and its people. Theo arrived back in the United States two weeks after Annette was born. I went to the airport to pick him up. I was late finding him at the airport because the name of his flight did not match any of the airlines on the arrival boards. I did not know the airline was a subsidiary of a major airline, and most of the counters were closed as it was the last flight to arrive.

When I finally located him, he was so angry.

"Where have you been?"

"I have been trying to locate the arrival gate. The name of the airline you gave me for your arrival does not appear on any arrival boards. I finally found someone to look it up and they gave me your arrival gate."

I continued pushing the stroller alongside Theo as we headed to the car. Annette, our two-week-old baby girl, was in the stroller, and I had it covered over with a baby blanket because she was sleeping.

"Do you want to see your daughter?

"No!"

"Why are you so upset and angry, other than it took me a while to find you?"

"The church fired me."

We found the car, and the entire drive back to the house where I was staying was silent. Theo did not want to talk, and I knew better than to try and get him to talk until he calmed down.

The church sent him back to be part of his new family. Theo was full of anger, as well as a host of other negative emotions. He continued to not want anything to do with Annette or me.

We subsequently moved out of the woman's house, where I had stayed for my entire pregnancy and until Theo arrived back in America. We moved into a one-bedroom apartment. The woman had given me her car to use until I could get a car of my own to get to and from work.

We went furniture shopping for the apartment. While looking at a sofa, Theo said, "This one will make a good bed."

"What do you mean it will make a good bed? We already picked out a bed."

"I'll be sleeping on the sofa."

The clues that my marriage was soon to be over were getting clearer and clearer day by day.

When Annette was two months old, we had arranged for Annette to be "blessed" in the church. When we got home from the blessing, Theo was sitting on the sofa (his bed). We were having another angry discussion, and I looked at him from the kitchen and said, "What, do you want a divorce?"

"Yes, I do!"

"Fine, I'll meet you at the courthouse tomorrow."

I could not deal with Theo's anger and feared for the safety of our daughter and myself. I had married Theo "for life" and should have fought for my marriage but I did not know who this man was that came back from Africa. The safety of Annette was more important to me than my marriage vows.

We met at the courthouse the next day, picked up the do-it-yourself divorce paperwork, and each filled out the requisite paperwork and filed it with the Court with me filing for divorce from Theo. Theo informed me he had gotten a job and was leaving town.

"What about the hearing date for the divorce?"

"You attend it. You're the one filing for a divorce. I do not need to be there."

With that, Theo walked out of the apartment with his personal belongings, and in less than a month, Theo and I were officially divorced. I stayed in touch with Theo during our five-year divorce. Our communication was pleasant but void of any intimacy or other details. When Theo was in town, he would sleep on "his" sofa and spend time with Annette; however, he had never even changed her diaper once.

Taking care of Annette and providing a loving and stable environment for her was a full-time job in addition to working full-time. Annette was in daycare for twelve hours a day, and that was enough stranger care for her. I did not have time for hobbies, sports, or activities because there was no one, including family members, that I could trust to take care of Annette at this stage. My mother was eighty-one years old and barely able to take care of herself, much less hold an infant.

Over time, I was able to get Theo to open up about his anger.

"You didn't have to deal with the questions regarding why you left so quickly, what did Judy do wrong, and how could they send her back to America and leave you here."

We did not discuss that anymore.

CHAPTER EIGHT–
THE BLESSED YEARS

GOD'S BLESSINGS AND
FRUITS OF THE SPIRIT

After Annette was born, I was determined to take financial steps to provide for Annette's college education. I had set up a special account that was paid monthly for tuition, room and board, and local fees.

Then, in December of 2006, after Theo and I got remarried, Theo was diagnosed with "inoperable cancer," as stated by four of the best surgeons in Miami. The fifth surgeon said, "I know I can save your husband's life." We scheduled the surgery. It was a long recovery; however, it was worth it.

Our finances took a major hit because Theo could no longer work. During our divorce, I bought a condominium with the income from my job and Theo's child support payments. Adjustments had to be made. Theo's youngest son had come to visit to help with his father's recovery. There were four of us living in a one-bedroom condo, and I could no longer afford it. We moved into an apartment that was cheaper and tried to sell the condominium during the worst mortgage fiasco in America. The bank would not accept two short sale contracts, and we eventually had to quit-claim the property back to the bank. All the appliances were stolen out of the unit during this time and there was nothing I could do. The management company had the keys to show the property and claimed they did not know when the appliances were stolen.

However, I must remember Proverbs 19:21 (NLT), "You can make many plans, but the Lord's purpose will prevail." I had to cancel Annette's prepaid college fund, cancel my life insurance, and make numerous other adjustments to survive. I was not sure how we'd survive financially, but we put our trust in God, who said he would give us abundant blessings—more than we could ever ask for.

When it came time for Annette to go to college, she excelled academically in the public schools, received credits for advanced classes and scholarships, and we did not have to pay for her tuition and books. She transferred to the university as a junior at the age of eighteen. We did pay for her to live in the dorm during her first year of university; however, COVID-19 happened, and she was sent home. She did not want to return to dorm life and finished her college career living at home.

God had provided again as he promised in Psalm 91 (NLT), "Those who live in the shelter of the Most High will find rest in the shadow of the Almighty. This I declare about the Lord: He alone is my refuge, my place of safety; he is my God, and I trust him. For he will rescue you from every trap and protect you from deadly disease. He will cover you with his feathers. He will shelter you with his wings. His faithful promises are your armor and protection. Do not be afraid of the terrors of the night, nor the arrow that flies in the day. Do not dread the disease that stalks in darkness, nor the disaster that strikes at midday. Though a thousand fall at your side, though ten thousand are dying around you, these evils will not touch you. Just open your eyes, and see how the wicked are punished. If you make the Lord your refuge, if you make the Most High your shelter, no evil will conquer you; no plague will come near your home. For he will order his angels to protect you wherever you go. They will hold you up with their hands so you won't even hurt your foot on a stone. You will trample upon lions and cobras; you will crush fierce lions and serpents under your feet! The Lord says, 'I will rescue those who love me. I will protect those who trust in my name. When they call on me, I will answer; I will be with them in trouble. I will rescue and honor them. I will reward them with a long life and give them my salvation.'"

There are so many times when I have felt so alone, afraid, not sure what the future holds, how I would pay for things, and whether I would be there to see Annette get married to a godly man, have children, and play with my grandchildren. When I spiritually see God, I see Him pulling me close to His body, wrapping His massive loving wings completely around me, and I feel unconditional love, peace, healing, strength, and protection.

When Theo was sixty-seven years old and Annette was a sixteen-year-old daughter, we decided to gamble on the United States economy and Annette's future, so we bought a just-our-size home and moved in. Homeownership, nicknamed part of the American dream, awakened God's Word to us each day in a fresh, new, living way over the past years. The weary-looking, tan-and-white, four-bedroom home looked quite ragged; however, in our eyes, it was a miracle from God blossoming from decades of prayers and goal setting.

Ten percent of the lawn had bits and pieces of grass; however, ninety percent of the front yard was home to clover leaves and yellow-flower weeds. I was convinced the entire wasp and honeybee population in our quaint little neighborhood was hovering on those flowers. On top of all that were lots of rock pieces, bits and pieces of white and yellow plastic bags, old, degraded cigarette and cigar butts, milk jugs and bottle caps, broken glass, and other unspeakable "garbage," covering the entire yard in the most disgraceful way. It was abundantly conspicuous that the home had no caretakers for a while and visitors did not regard it as a home.

I saw our yard as representing the lost, lonely, and struggling individuals of the world trying to navigate the stings and dangers of life with no one protecting or watching over them and being dumped on by those who were supposed to be their friends.

Being like most cash-strapped, new homeowners, we decided our first mission involved putting on extra heavy-duty gloves, picking up debris, pulling weeds and turning the soil, spreading healthy, heat-friendly grass seed in a hand-cranked seeder, and watering with a too-short garden hose connected to the side of the house. We did all this while baking for hours in the hot, skin-blistering sun. For our reward, we set up plastic white chairs on our front porch slab so we could enjoy our new home and watch our grass grow over the following days.

Sadly, most of the seeds fell into the roots of the weeds, and the weeds choked the life out of them, or the birds carried the seed away for food. Some of the seeds fell on rocky soil, and when the sun came up, it burned the seed, which had no root and withered away. There were a couple of places where the seed fell into good ground and brought forth this spiny-looking chunk of grass; however, it was nothing like what we wanted it to be.

Our soil, like my innermost foundation, needed to be tilled and ready to properly receive and grow to its full potential. I had been attending church and praying; however, most of the messages became entwined in strong, well-rooted weeds in my life or carried away by individuals who had no interest in my growth. I knew those weeds needed to be ripped up, broken, and destroyed. Other messages received with joy and enthusiasm made me believe I would immediately turn 180 degrees and change my errant behavior, except when the first perceived persecution or tribulation appeared, I forgot that message and fell back into my weed-infested, self-pitying world. The slightest prick to my self-esteem would bring out my true human nature. Oh, what a wretch I was!

We broke down and realized some serious pruning was involved. We rented a tiller, ripped, pulled, raked, and removed objects that didn't belong, and ordered some wonderful, resilient golf-course variety sod. We did not live near a beautiful stream or river; however, Home Depot sold some great sprinklers that looked like streams of water flowing in the air. The sod arrived, the watering began, and the yard was lush and full, and the mowing was now in full gear. The start of summer has arrived, and within two days of not watering, our sod begins to wither. It is at that point that we realized in order to rescue the sod, we must begin watering it again.

I too needed that watering. Therefore, I started attending a new, good, old-fashioned, neighborhood church, which is leading, guiding, and worshiping from the Word. My hidden seeds that were placed in the good ground when I was born again years ago have begun bearing fruit again. To keep bearing fruit, my fruit needs to be properly pruned, and through trials and tribulations, I know that God will keep it grounded to its foundation.

God's fruit was growing in my life. Every day for almost two years, Annette and I would ride the train together. She was going to high school and college while I was going to work. We were on a tight schedule. After a while, you meet people on the train who roll on the same schedule as you do. We met this woman who worked at the state courthouse. She was always cheerful and polite, quiet and reserved, and a joy to speak with.

Then, for a long time, she was not seen, and one bright morning, she appeared. She had knee surgery and was doing rehabilitation. We talked as if no time had been missed, discussing her health and discussing Annette, who had since graduated high school with her diploma and AA degree at the same time and transferred to university to complete her bachelor's degree.

A couple of days later, I went to work in a pair of khaki pants. When I got to work, I noticed that there were black marks and stains all over my pants. It was still early enough in the morning that no one at work had seen me yet. I worked in downtown Miami, and I immediately ran over to Ross Stores to buy a new pair of pants.

When I was coming out of the changing room, a young woman asked me, "Don't you ride the train with your teenage daughter?"

I replied, "Yes."

"I have watched the two of you for months on the train together. You were always having so much fun together. It was so refreshing to see a mother and daughter that close."

In addition to knowing that God is always watching us and watching over us, it confirms the belief that other people are watching you because the light of Christ is emitting from within, even when you do not realize it, and your actions are being noticed and judged.

"SENSE" YOU LOVED ME

For the past thirteen years, I have worked in Big Law as a legal secretary, and every Friday, this humble, quiet woman would bring a colorful variety of flowers to buy.

The flowers are all different varieties, sizes, and colors. All colors of the rainbow are fully represented. My favorite flower has always been a hybrid combination of red and orange carnations, which reminds me of wood crackling and snapping with flickering flames in a fireplace.

I used to buy these flowers and take them home to entice my visual and nasal senses; however, my four rambunctious cats enjoyed my flowers in a different manner than me.

They would eat the flowers off the end of the stems. If they were hungry for greens, why didn't they eat the leaves and not the flowers?

I would come home and, looking through my financially colored, green eyes, get angry with my cats. I was yelling at four of God's creatures whose sole existence in our house is to provide unconditional love and hours of enjoyment, watching them live and play without a care in the world.

I stopped buying flowers, and every Friday, when the woman would ask me if I was going to buy any flowers, I would have to say no, as that day became a reminder of sadness rather than joy.

Then, in 2017, little did I know my world would change completely. Theo, Annette, and I moved into our new home. Theo, my husband of thirty-four years really was paying attention to me all those years because one of the first things he did was buy and plant a hybrid hibiscus bush in our front yard.

We did not even have grass in our front yard, but we had a hibiscus bush. Now, this was not just any hibiscus bush; this was a fire hibiscus bush. Over the past year, that single-fire hibiscus bush has been joined by five other multiple-colored, hybrid hibiscus bushes.

Every day, on at least one of the hibiscus bushes, there are flowers, and most days, there are several. God brings me flowers every single day if only I will look and see.

When I go and relax and share time with my family on our front porch in our plastic, white chairs and take time to see with God's eyes, I see He brings me beautiful multi-colored flowers, the smell of Citronella in the bush in front of our porch; the large green lizards who have taken up residence in our yard and enjoy running through the soft, vividly green, Zoysia grass, or running through the mulch in the hibiscus garden; the singing starlings who God feeds daily with worms or bugs maneuvering through the mulch, or the woodpecker who returns daily to his telephone pole to make sure his home is safe and predator-free; the flock of ibis flying over in v-formation, the young children playing carefree at the little community park across the street; and the peace of knowing that God provides all those sensory items if only I would stop long enough to see, hear, smell, touch, and taste the magnificence of His world.

I never bought roses, nor wanted roses in my yard, because they had taken on such a significance at my church. Every Mother's Day, my church would use roses to remind us of God's greatest sacrifice through a somber but loving reflection. Each woman received roses; a red rose for every mother still alive, i.e., mother, mother-in-law, maternal mother, or paternal mother, and a white rose for every mother who passed on. My mother passed on, and I never met my grandmother or my mother-in-law. However, every Mother's Day, I reflect on how much I miss my mother, who passed over in February 2007. I loved her even though she wasn't the best mom, but I knew she was the mom God picked out for me.

Psalm 139:13 (NIV) says, "For you created my inmost being; you knit me together in my mother's womb." Just as God had knit me in my mother's womb, I know God knit Annette together in my womb. The significance of the red rose versus the white rose takes on greater meaning around Easter time. The blood of Christ is available for mothers still alive. For the ones who have passed over, Christ will share the last cup of wine from the Seder with them in heaven.

Ephesians 3:20 (AMP) tells me, "Now to Him who is able to [carry out His purpose and] do superabundantly more than all that we dare ask or think [infinitely beyond our greatest prayers, hopes, or dreams], according to His power that is at work within us." Therefore, I pray that Annette and I will have lots of time to share the blood of Jesus before either one of us passes over.

CHAPTER NINE–
THE MOUNTAIN YEARS

THE PAINFUL GROWTH
OF ADULTHOOD

"I won't be coming home this weekend," said Annette, my eighteen-year-old daughter.

I knew Annette was not dead, but I felt like someone had gut-punched me. The overwhelming sadness was too much, and my tears started flowing like a waterfall. My little girl, now an independent, no-nonsense woman, had just moved into a four-quad-bedroom dorm.

Theo and I thought it would be best if Annette experienced living on her own for a while. We did not want her to become dependent on us as she was already independent, and we wanted her to gain confidence.

We told Annette that if she needed us at any time, day or night, we'd be there for her, and we were.

There were nights she just wanted to sleep in her own bed, and we would pick her up and we would take her back the next morning. She did great caring for herself, doing laundry, grocery shopping, cooking, cleaning, and figuring out how to live with roommates she did not know prior to entering the dorm. In March 2020, COVID-19 happened, and she was sent home. We all were incredibly happy.

As my Annette matured, I remembered one of the lessons I was taught about judgment being a two-way street.

I woke up one morning still reeling from the sting of words spoken the night before. "No, you are wrong! Just leave her alone with what she said."

Theo was standing up for Annette against me. This was not the first time this had happened, and lately, it seemed to be happening more and more.

I broke the cardinal rule in marriage and life, "Be ye angry, and sin not: let not the sun go down upon your wrath." (Ephesians 4:26, KJV). I took my blood-red face to bed to mask my hurt and anger. As soon as my head hit the pillow, my anger turned to tears, quietly sobbing so no one in the house would hear.

I pleaded my case with God about how righteous I was in my position and God heard and replied.

My scripture reading the next morning was about forgiving others as Jesus had forgiven me. Then, I read the Word of the Day. "No weapon that is formed against thee shall prosper; and every tongue that shall rise against thee in judgment thou shalt condemn. This is the heritage of the servants of the Lord, and their righteousness is of me, saith the Lord." (Isaiah 54:17, KJV).

I felt so righteous and uplifted and was ready to face the day. I decided I would forgive Theo and Annette for saying the hurtful things they said because of Christ's love for me.

I felt reassured that no weapon formed against me shall prosper, including those guided, heart-seeking missiles from the night before. But something still did not feel "right."

I knew this scripture. I relied on it for strength to sustain me in tough situations. What was God trying to teach me? I re-read the Word of the Day.

Somewhere in my learning, memorizing, and using this scripture, I inadvertently omitted the words that read, "Every tongue that shall rise against thee in judgment thou shalt condemn."

My tongue had risen against Theo and Annette with judgment rather than love.

God, please forgive me!

Finally, I realized my anger was prideful! My pride caused my anger and judgment against *them*! I had set up my own condemnation!

Only through repentance and asking Jesus for forgiveness does God release me from that condemnation. How many times have I gotten angry at someone for hurting *me*? How many times have I stood firm in my righteousness and judged *them*? Romans 2:1 (TLV) says, "Therefore you are without excuse, O man—every one of you who is judging. For by whatever you judge another, you condemn yourself. For you who judge practice the same things."

God, please show me how to humbly love another when I do not agree with their words or perspective. Show me how to move forward in grace and mercy, which You have freely given to me through Jesus Christ. Amen.

There are days I wonder where Shaggy is; however, I know that Shaggy is the wrong place to go. These thoughts are not from God!

YOU'RE NOT DONE YET

Theo had just completed his pre-op appointments. We were hopeful as we prepared to go to his surgical oncologist to schedule his surgery to finally remove his retroperitoneal liposarcoma that had returned after fourteen years. After great difficulty getting his seventy-year-old, extremely painful, over-bloated, catheterized body to the car, we got him into the passenger seat, and I jumped around to the driver's seat to take off. He said, "I need to go to the bathroom."

I turned the car off and went around to the passenger's side to help him out. His head fell back against the headrest, and he appeared to have passed out. I yelled at him.

"Theo, wake up! Theo, wake up!"

I slapped his face a few times, not worried about the consequences. I do not know how long I tried to revive him. I just kept slapping him and yelling at him.

"Theo, pay attention!"

Finally, his eyes started opening and rolling back in his head, and he was coming around. I raced to the ring doorbell and pushed it. Annette came out, and I yelled at her, "Call 911!"

She immediately called 911, and I could hear her speaking to them in the background. I went back to the car with her following behind.

Theo finally woke up. I had managed to get one leg out of the car before he passed out and was now pushing it back into the car until fire rescue showed up. Theo quietly asked.

"What happened?"

"You passed out."

Fire rescue arrived, and I stepped away. They examined Theo, and he was talking with them. They asked me what I wanted to do.

"I want him to go to the hospital. We were on our way to the oncologist, and he just passed out."

"Well, he is awake now, so it isn't your choice. It is his choice. He does not want to go to the hospital. He wants to go to his oncologist. He appears okay. It's probably best to take him to his appointment because if his oncologist thinks he should be in the hospital, he can make arrangements for him to be admitted."

"We will do that. Thank you."

Fire rescue left. Annette had a class she had to attend and could not go with us to the doctor.

"Annette, I am going to take him to the doctor. I will call you when I find out anything."

We arrived at the oncologist's office. I grabbed the walker out of the back seat of the car and managed to get Theo to sit on the walker. He had deteriorated so fast over these past three months that we got him a walker because he could no longer walk unassisted. He would sit on the walker, and I would push him around. I pushed him through the long corridors to the elevator and up to the second floor, pushed him through the office doors, and checked him in.

"Theo, we're ready for you." We were led into the examination room. The doctor and two resident PAs warmly greeted us. This is the same physician who saved Theo's life fourteen years prior, and I'm resting all my hopes on God and him to do it again.

"How are you doing, Theo?" asked the doctor. Theo says, "I'm here to schedule my surgery."

I chime in.

"Yesterday, Theo's leg began ulcerating, and I've bandaged them to the best of my ability."

The doctor looks at Theo's legs and states,

"There is too much fluid in the legs, and these are ulcers. I will bandage them." He asks the PAs to get the necessary bandages for the legs. In the meantime, he wants to know how the cardiology and pulmonary appointments went.

Theo replied, "I passed all the tests with no problems."

"Doctor, Theo passed out in the car on the way to this appointment. I called Fire Rescue, and he was revived by the time they arrived. Theo refused to go to the hospital, and they said to bring him here, and you could decide what was best for Theo."

"Well, Theo, your vitals are a little out of whack; however, he appears fine. I can hospitalize you to take care of these ulcers and make you a little more comfortable; however, there is nothing else I can do for you."

"Well, while I'm in the hospital, can you do the surgery?"

"No, I am sorry, Theo, that surgery is out of the question, given your current state. There is nothing else I can do for you."

My heart sank to my feet and Theo's face went sheet white.

"What do you mean?

"There is nothing more I can do for you. Your condition is beyond any medical intervention other than hospice. I can put you in the hospital to help with the ulcers and then place you in hospice when you get out, or I can place you in hospice now. What would you like me to do?"

After about ten minutes of trying to understand what was just said, Theo said, "No hospital, just put me on hospice, as long as they will give me something for the pain and something to help me sleep."

"My orders will include something for the pain and something for sleep."

We left that appointment where I was at the point of tears; however, I had to be strong for Theo. His world had just crumbled.

On the drive home, Theo kept saying in tears,

"I'm so sorry. I had no idea I had gotten this bad."

"Annette and I knew you were and that is why we were so angry at you when you checked out of the hospital AMA (absent medical authorization) three weeks ago. Your surgery was scheduled for four days later. Then we had that hit-and-run accident on the way home from the hospital, and I was not sure if you were injured further."

I grabbed his leg, and he grabbed my hand, and I said, "We will figure this out. It will be okay somehow."

When we got home, we explained the situation to Annette. She had already surmised this would be the case. She was so strong. She immediately started chatting with her father while I made the necessary arrangements.

I called the hospice care agency and set up an appointment for 7:30 a.m. the next morning for them to bring all of the necessary equipment to make Theo's life easier in the living room, as he was almost completely unable to walk anymore and the hallways in our house were too narrow and couldn't accommodate a walker or wheelchair.

To this day, Annette and I are certain that Theo died earlier in the car. We believe that God knew Theo had left things undone in this world, and he allowed Theo to come back to put things in order. The following events happened, which confirmed beyond a reasonable doubt that God had told Theo, "You're not done yet!"

As soon as we got home, Theo said, "I need to speak with a pastor today."

"Theo, your pastor at your church retired a couple of years ago, and I do not know how to get in touch with him. I could try and locate him on the internet. Would you like to speak with my pastor?"

"Yes."

My pastor had met and spoken briefly with Theo once. I immediately called my pastor and filled him in on Theo's condition, and he agreed to speak with Theo. I gave Theo my phone and went outside to sit on the front porch and pray. I wanted Theo to have all the privacy he wanted to get himself right with God. About an hour later, my daughter came out and told me I could come back in. Theo was in surprisingly good spirits. It was now dinner time and we decided to order one of our favorite meals, sushi, for dinner.

"Would you like to watch a movie with dinner?" asked Theo.

The food arrived, we ate, we watched the movie, we laughed, we talked, and we thoroughly enjoyed ourselves. We went to bed around 12:30 a.m., as Annette had a 7:30 a.m. final exam, and I had to go to work. Theo went to sleep in his sofa recliner, which had become his bed for about two months.

"Mom, I think Dad's dead," said Annette grimly as I looked up from a sound sleep.

I jumped out of bed, raced to the living room, and saw Theo slumped over in his chair. It was 3:50 a.m. He was not breathing. I started screaming,

"Call 911. Put them on the speaker. I think my husband's dead. He's not breathing."

"Where is he?"

"He's in the sofa recliner chair."

"Pull him out of the chair onto the ground and start CPR?"

"He is too heavy. We cannot get him out of the chair."

"Does the chair recline?"

"Yes."

"Well, lay it all the way back and start CPR. Fire rescue is on the way."

We started CPR and continued until fire rescue arrived. They looked at Theo, listened to his heart, tried to take a pulse, and said,

"I'm sorry, he's gone."

Annette and I were in shock.

"Now, what I asked? Where will you take him?"

"Nowhere. You need to have someone remove the body. We will stay here until the body is removed."

"Who do I call?"

"Did your husband have a will, or did you discuss funeral arrangements?"

"Yes, he wanted to be cremated."

"Then you can call a crematorium, and they will pick up the body."

"Are there any open at this hour?"

I started searching the internet and located a twenty-four-hour crematorium and called them.

"My husband has passed away. He wanted to be cremated, and we needed to have the body removed. The police are here now, and they will not leave until the body is removed."

After settling the initial charges, they agreed to come over and take the body. The crematorium arrived. They loaded the body on the gurney and covered it with clear plastic. I do not know why it was clear; however, our Ring video took pictures of the body being wheeled out and wheeled to the van, and that would be the last we would see of Theo in this world.

My daughter and I knew that this was just the shell of her father and my husband because we knew that Theo was already with Jesus, and they were both looking down on us, smiling as we managed one of the most difficult times in our lives.

It was now close to 7:00 a.m. and Annette went to her room to prepare for her final exam. She had to take this exam because the professor had already said, "If you do not take this exam, you will fail my class." This was her last class for that semester at college and one of her last exams.

Annette was scheduled to graduate with her B.A. in chemistry on May 7, 2022, at the age of twenty. Her father died on April 14, 2021.

Annette and I knew she had worked too hard, getting her AA degree, before getting her high school diploma at seventeen years old, to have it all crumble at such a crucial moment. She would take the exam and accept whatever grade she received.

I followed Annette back to her room.

"What made you wake up at that hour and go check on Dad?"

Normally, it was my job to wake up every couple of hours and check on Theo sleeping in the chair.

"The house was too quiet."

Theo was so sick near the end that he coughed 24/7. It had been that way for the last few months; however, this time, he finally stopped coughing, and the silence woke her up.

Annette took her final exam.

I called my office and told them, "Theo died this morning. I will not be coming to work today."

When Annette finished her exam, we sat together in the living room, piecing together our last day with Theo on earth. We know we will see him again with Christ.

When I am sad or lonely, I turn on Christian music and let the music express my feelings and allow me to worship God because He is the only one who can dry my tears and fill up my broken heart. MercyMe wrote a song called "Word of God Speak," and whenever I sing the lyrics, I know I'm really crying out to God, telling Him I don't know what to say. I only want to hear Him speak to me in His quiet voice. I want Him to cleanse my eyes and ears to see and hear His glory and majesty. I want to be still and know that He is with me wherever I am. I want to just sit and stay with Him and know that all I need is to be with Him.

Then I spiritually see myself wrapped up again in God's wings, and everything is okay. Thank You, God. You have spoken.

Shortly after Theo passed away and Annette had finished her semester, Annette and I decided to take a road trip to see my brother in Tallahassee, Florida, with Annette driving. Annette and I do not like a lot of traffic; therefore, we do our road trips at night.

We were about an hour outside of Miami, taking an exit ramp from I-95 to the Turnpike. It was a two-lane exit ramp, and to the left of us was a tow truck with a vehicle on its bed. As we headed into the curve, I told Annette that the tow truck was taking the curve too fast and the vehicle on its bed was not properly secured. I was married to a professional truck driver for many years. Theo had shown me when a load was properly secured when I traveled with him on vacation for two weeks in the truck back in the 1980s. This vehicle was only secured by the front axle. We saw the back end of the towed vehicle slide to the right and the tow truck swerving into our lane from the load shift. I cannot explain it physically, but supernaturally, I saw this huge hand come between the tow truck and the left side of our vehicle, protecting us from colliding. I *know* this was the Hand of God.

As if that was not confirmation enough of God telling us, "You're not done yet, either," several hours later into the trip, we were passing a tractor-trailer that appeared to either get distracted or fall asleep at the wheel and started coming into our lane. There was nowhere for us to go as there was a wall on the left side of us. Again, I saw this huge Hand of God come between the two of us on the right side of the vehicle and gently push the tractor-trailer back into his lane. God was protecting Annette and me.

From that moment on, I knew that God's plan for my life was to write this book about twice, supernaturally, "Seeing the Hand of God," on our road trip, as well as seeing His Hand continually guiding me and protecting me throughout my lifetime, even when I didn't supernaturally see it.

IT'S STAGE 3

In January 2021, I went for my yearly gynecological appointment slightly later due to the COVID-19 lockdown. I was told that everything looked good and told to get my mammogram.

In April of 2021, Theo passed away, and Annette and I had not really had a chance to grieve his loss; however, we kept moving forward to the best of our ability.

In May of 2021, I had my mammogram, and while I was waiting for them to tell me my images were good and that they would get back to me with the results, I was ushered into a private room.

"Your films are showing highly suspect findings, and we need you to have a biopsy immediately. Here is the phone number of a doctor who can do a biopsy." I prayed to God and hoped for the best.

I scheduled the extremely painful biopsy for May 14, 2021, a month to the day after Theo died. It was confirmed—stage 3 breast cancer. I remember praying Psalm 23 (KJV): "The LORD is my shepherd; I shall not want. He maketh me to lie down in green pastures: He leadeth me beside the still waters. He restoreth my soul: He leadeth me in the paths of righteousness for his name's sake. Yea, though I walk through the valley of the shadow of death, I will fear no evil: for thou art with me; Thy rod and thy staff they comfort me. Thou preparest a table before me in the presence of mine enemies: Thou anointest my head with oil; my cup runneth over. Surely goodness and mercy shall follow me all the days of my life: And I will dwell in the house of the LORD for ever."

At the appointment to begin treatment, the medical oncologist said, "We need to start chemotherapy to attempt to shrink the eight cm large tumor in your right breast, which appears to have infiltrated into your lymph nodes." Annette was with me for the appointment. It was the only time she was allowed into the appointment due to COVID-19.

"Why can't we just do surgery right away to remove the tumor? How could something this large grow in my breast when four months earlier, the OB/GYN did not feel anything?"

"We need you to do six months of infused chemotherapy to try to shrink the tumor and to attempt to stop any further infiltration through the lymph nodes. You will need to have a port inserted for the infusion. We have no way of knowing if this has metastasized at this point. After the chemotherapy, we will reevaluate, and we will do the surgery followed by radiation."

I had not even had a chance to grieve the loss of my husband, and now this. Annette was my helper through all of this. Annette would drive me to the hospital for my chemotherapy, which would take about four to five hours each time, and she would have to sit in the car due to COVID-19 and do her college studies.

In addition to this, my OB/GYN had found an unusual finding in my uterus, and I underwent a hysteroscopy in May to make sure there was nothing wrong there. Those results were negative.

I was still working full-time throughout the six months of chemotherapy, in addition to numerous visits for blood workups to make sure my body was managing the killing concoction.

"The tumor has shrunk, and the affected lymph nodes have shrunk, and we think you are ready for surgery. You have the option of only doing one radical mastectomy of your right breast with lymph nodes; however, there is no way of knowing if the cancer has spread."

"I want a double radical mastectomy of both breasts, and I don't want any reconstruction. My husband is dead, and I do not see myself with any other man."

I had surgery, removing both breasts and lymph nodes from the left side and major lymph removal on the right side. They removed five lymph node clusters from the right side with active cancer in the first four lymph nodes.

I was ready to go back to work two weeks later; however, my

employer did not want me back until after I had completed my radiation treatment and physical therapy, which was scheduled to start in December and was a daily occurrence for about four weeks. The physical therapy was for my right arm as I had lost a lot of range of motion after the surgery due to tissue and lymph nodes being removed from that side.

After the radiation, I was told that due to my aggressive cancer and the fact that there is no way to know if the cancer made it past the lymph nodes, I would need to take oral chemotherapy for at least the next two years and hormone therapy for the next five to ten years. My body did not like oral chemotherapy. After about four months of horrible side effects from the chemotherapy, the medical oncologist reduced the dosage in half, figuring it was better to take half the dosage than have my body reject the full dosage, negating any long-term benefits.

I returned to work full-time in January of 2022 and continue to work to the present. All my vacation and sick time goes for follow-up visits and treatments. My employer has been wonderful, emotionally supportive, and understanding.

God continues to show me that by the blood of Jesus, I am healed. All my results have continued to report good findings like no change in bone density. Annette and I changed our diet to a professional food service and my doctors are impressed by my blood work getting better all the time.

Printed in the USA
CPSIA information can be obtained
at www.ICGtesting.com
CBHW071531260724
12259CB00009B/113

9 798893 330793